KASHGAR
OASIS CITY ON CHINA'S OLD SILK ROAD

KASHGAR

OASIS CITY ON CHINA'S OLD SILK ROAD

Photographs by John Gollings

Introduction by

George Michell, Marika Vicziany and Tsui Yen Hu

FRANCES LINCOLN LIMITED

PUBLISHERS

Frances Lincoln Ltd
4 Torriano Mews
Torriano Avenue
London NW5 2RZ
www.franceslincoln.com

Half Title: A merchant surrounded by metallic wares and ropes in Kashgar's Old City.
Title page: Two dear lady friends who share a house in the Old City.
These pages: Snowy peaks of the Tienshan range on the edge of the Kashgar Oasis.

CONTENTS

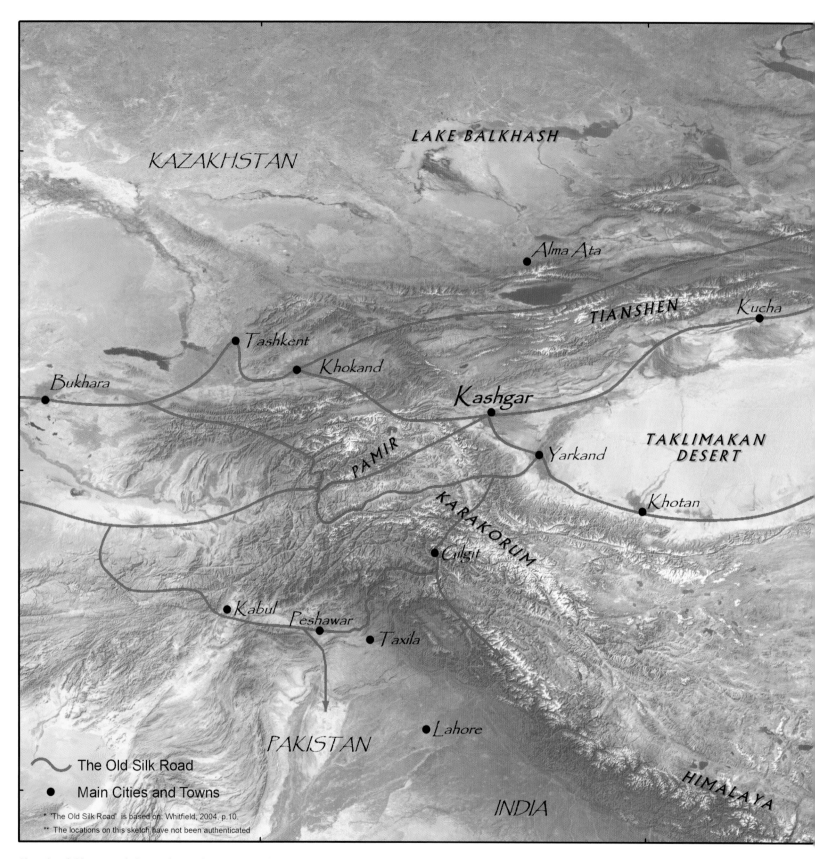

Sketch of China and Central Asia locating Kashgar on the Old Silk Road.

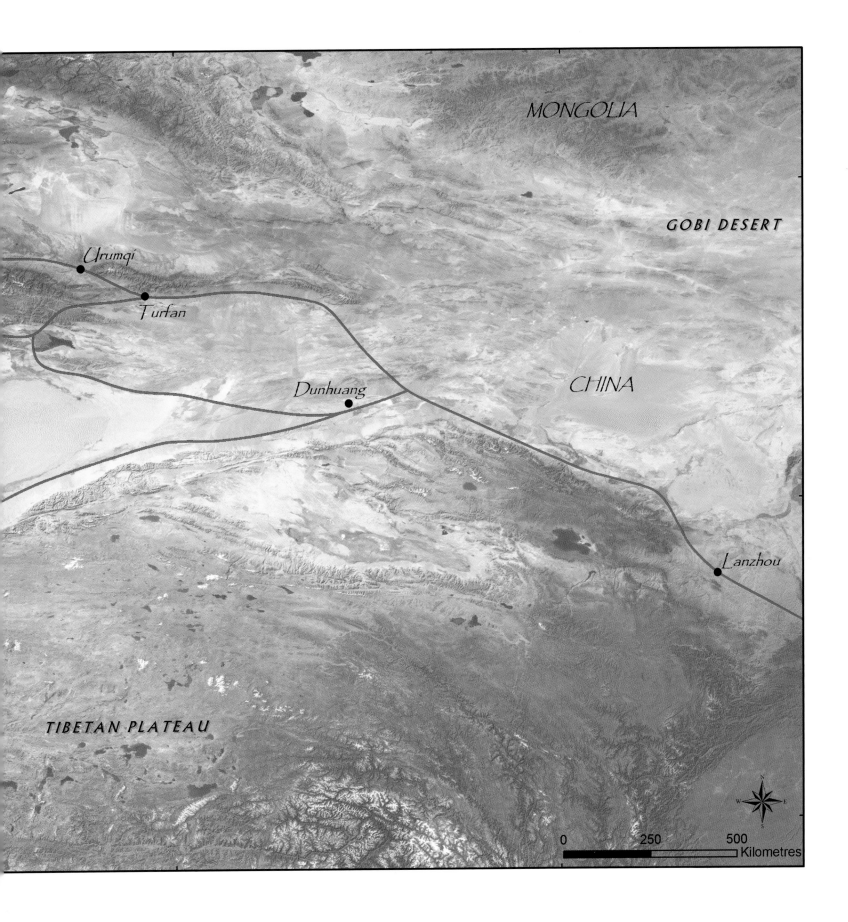

MONGOLIA

GOBI DESERT

Urumqi

Turfan

Dunhuang

CHINA

Lanzhou

TIBETAN PLATEAU

0   250   500
▭ Kilometres

MAP 7

INTRODUCTION

John Gollings's panorama of the old city of Kashgar dominated by a colossal statue of Mao, one arm lifted in salute, exemplifies the meeting of present and the past in this extreme south-west corner of the People's Republic of China.

More than 4,000 kilometres distant from Beijing, and no less than 1,500 kilometres from Urumqi, capital of the Xinjiang Uygur Autonomous Region in which it is now situated, Kashgar may seem at first to be a remote destination, far from the main centres of power and commerce in eastern China. But up until the early decades of the twentieth century Kashgar enjoyed the reputation of being the 'pivot' of Central Asia, since it was one of the principal nodes along the great Silk Road which linked China with the Middle East and the Mediterranean, as well as the Indian Subcontinent to the south.

Inhabited through the centuries by successive waves of peoples professing Buddhist, Manichaean, Nestorian and Zoroastrian beliefs, Kashgar eventually became home to Uygur migrants from the Mongolian heartland to the north;[1] it is the mainly the descendants of these people who live there today, though the city has also attracted peoples from neighbouring Tajikistan, Kyrgyzstan and Afghanistan, as well as from the Chinese heartland to the east. It survives today as the most complete, historical urban centre in Xinjiang. The densely packed houses and narrow lanes of Kashgar's old city, dotted with mosques and madrasas, stalls and markets, are home to a society that is still traditionally Muslim. Kashgar's celebrated Sunday Market is the most vibrant in the whole region. Here more than anywhere else in Central Asia, the cosmopolitan spirit of the Old Silk Road is still very much alive.

KASHGAR IN HISTORY

Kashgar, known in old European maps as Cascar, has been ruled by so many tribes, clans, warriors, priests and soldiers of fortune that its dense history is almost incomprehensible to a first-time visitor. Even the name of Kashgar is contested: contemporary travel agencies talk of Kashi, which is the official Chinese name for Kashgar, but the Chinese annals call it Shule. What visitors need to grasp is the unique location of this oasis city and why its green mantle has provided such relief to the

sand-blown faces of countless visitors approaching from so many different directions. The historical significance of Kashgar is best understood from its situation on the edge of the Taklimakan desert in the middle of the Tarim Basin, in what was once known as Chinese Turkestan. The routes of long-distance trade that in the past made up the Old Silk Road skirted around this inhospitable wasteland, converging on the Kashgar oasis before making their way through the passes of the formidable mountains that surround the city on three sides. This ongoing traffic of goods, cultures and religions underscores the lucrative career of the city's merchants and markets over a period of no less than two thousand years.

Kashgar first enters history in the second century CE, when it was the headquarters of a Hinayana sect of Buddhism, with a huge community of monks and several hundreds of temples. In addition to being an active centre of Buddhism, Kashgar was known at this time for its fine carpets of wool. From the fourth to the eighth centuries Kashgar, together with most of the Tarim Basin, was absorbed into the Manichaean Soghdian kingdom of neighbouring Transoxiana, in present-day Uzbekistan. The commercial networks established by the Soghdians connected Kashgar with Iran to the west, the kingdom of Bactria in the Upper Indus valley to the south and the empire of the Tang Chinese to the east. Among the precious goods that were traded along the Old Silk Road at this time were silver, gold, wine, pepper, camphor and musk.

However, by the seventh century the Chinese had asserted their influence in the region, and in 657 the Tang emperor of China installed a local Turkic khan to govern the Tarim Basin in his name.[2] In the following century the Arabs arrived on the extreme western periphery of the Tang Empire. The battle of Talas River in present-day Kyrgyzstan in 751 is remembered as the first as well as the last confrontation of the Arab and Chinese armies.

Though the Arabs never settled in the Tarim Basin, their Islamic religion spread steadily throughout the region, especially among the Uygur Turkic people of Mongolia, who began to migrate into the region from the ninth century onwards. In spite of their gradual conversion to Islam, the Uygurs retained aspects of their earlier shamanistic beliefs which had prevailed during their time as nomads in Mongolia, as well as retaining aspects of their attachment to Manichaeism, which had been

declared to be the state religion of the Uygur empire in Mongolia (745–840). Once settled in the Kashgar region, the Uygurs rapidly rose to power, governing as the Qarakhanid dynasty from the tenth to the twelfth centuries. The Qarakhanid dynasty had two capitals: Kashgar was the winter palace and Balasaghun, in modern Kyrgyzstan, was the summer palace.

The most prominent figure from this era is Mahmud Kashgari, who attained fame as compiler of the first Turkic dictionary, written in Baghdad in the last decades of the eleventh century.[3] Mahmud travelled between the religious colleges of the Tarim Basin and the Tigri–Euphrates Valley, and his career testifies to the stimulating cultural exchanges that occurred along the Old Silk Road. His tomb in the Kashgar oasis, near Opal, remains a popular pilgrimage destination to this day. Throughout this period, despite cultural exchange with the Islamic heartlands the culture of Kashgar tolerated a wide variety of beliefs, only one of which was Islam.

From the thirteenth century onwards the Tarim Basin came under the sway successively of Chinggis Khan of Mongolia, Timur (Tamerlane) of Samarqand in Central Asia and the emperors of the Ming dynasty in the Chinese heartland to the east. Kashgar continued to prosper, thanks to the city's role as a significant entrepôt between China and the Muslim world. This era also witnessed the activities of a number of Sufi teachers and saints, especially those of the Naqshbandi order, who continued the task of Islamicizing the population of the Tarim Basin.

The increased prosperity of Kashgar meant that various military figures from the neighbouring lands attempted to assert their authority over the city and the other towns of the oasis. The most successful of these were the Khojas, who emerged as khans of Kashgar in the course of the sixteenth century. Acting as emissaries of Islamic Sufism, the Khojas justified their rise to power by claiming to be rightful descendants of the Prophet Muhammad, in particular the children of Ali and Fatima. The best known of these figures was Apa Khoja, who ruled in the second half of the seventeenth century. His memory is still very much alive in Kashgar today, judging from the crowds of devotees who visit his tomb on the outskirts of the city. In the following years the Tarim Basin, including the Kashgar Oasis, came under the administration of the Chinese Qing emperors, who took pains to maintain garrisons in the region.

By the early nineteenth century Kashgar and Yarkand, the second largest city of the region, had begun to attract the ambitions of warlords from the kingdom of Khokand in the neighbouring Ferghana valley, in present-day Uzbekistan. One of the most successful of these figures was Yaqub Beg, who wrested control of Kashgar and its oasis from the Chinese. Yaqub Beg was unusual in that he managed to rule for some ten years (1866–77) in an era when contenders came and went as quickly as pigeons in flight to the next adventure spot. Despite the relative stability of his regime, what Yaqub Beg represented remains ambiguous; we do not even know whether he was ethnically Tajik, Uzbek or Turkic. The one thing we can be certain of is that he was a successful warlord and came to Kashgar on a mission to relieve it of its wealth in order to support the court of Khokand.[4] His military successes gave way to personal ambition, and he quickly established himself as a local potentate. As unpredictable as the shifting sands of the Taklimakan, Yaqub Beg's reign ushered in a decade of reconstruction that was compatible with Islamic values and law.

Meanwhile agents of the Russian and British Empires began extending their influence into the region, though their intrusions were resisted for a time by Yaqub Beg and the Qing military governors. It was these events that ushered in the era of the Great Game,[5] during which Russian and British ambitions confronted each other by establishing a presence in Kashgar itself, which by now was considered the 'pivot' of Central Asia. In the end, however, the Qing administration prevailed, its supremacy hastened by Yaqub Beg's fatal stroke during a major military campaign in 1877.

The Great Game established a new era of international diplomacy that lasted into the 1920s and 1930s. Xinjiang's trade with the Soviet Union came to dominate the local economy, while Soviet political interference contributed to the warlordism that increasingly came to characterize the Kashgar region in the period up to the Second World War. Another important outcome of the expansion of Soviet power towards China's border during the 1920s and 1930s was that many of the most important Sufi leaders fled Central Asia and escaped to Xinjiang, Pakistan and Afghanistan, thereby reinvigorating Sufism in western China.

For some months in 1933 and 1934 proclamations were made about a new Chinese Turkestan Republic, but these did not produce any viable results. They did, however, reaffirm the centrality of Kashgar for Muslim Uygurs, as these movements had their base in that city. Chaos and confusion eventually gave way in 1949 to a rejection of the Chinese nationalists. Kashgar, together with the whole of the Tarim Basin, sided with the Chinese Communist Party in a complex political negotiation that led to the formation of the Xinjiang Uygur Autonomous Region in 1955.

THE UYGURS

The word 'Uygur' means 'to join or form an alliance', referring to the era when Uygurs formed themselves into nomadic Turkic confederations. About three-quarters of Kashgar's 400,000 citizens are Uygur Muslims, and Uygurs also represent the majority of the rural population in the Kashgar Oasis; together they account for the largest concentration of these people to be found anywhere in Xinjiang. As a result, Uygur linguistic, cultural and social traditions dominate the life of Kashgar and much of its surroundings.

Geographically, the Uygurs came from Mongolia, but their cultural and linguistic identity was Turkic, and closely related to that of their Tajik, Kyrgyz and Uzbek neighbours, who also converted to Islam from the tenth century onwards. In this regard, Kashgar's population forms part of a greater Central Asian Muslim world that is linked historically with the long-standing traffic of the Old Silk Road. The numerous signs in Persian script that appear over shops and offices on the main streets of Kashgar reveal the linguistic affiliation of the city's population, even though most educated Uygurs are also fluent in Mandarin, the official language.

As in other communities in Muslim Central Asia, class dominates Uygur society. Kashgar still has a Khoja elite which regards itself as cultured and privileged, and the direct descendants from the Khoja court of earlier times. Highly born Khoja ladies of the city tend to be fully veiled in light materials and prefer not to venture outside their homes. Thanks to their frequent and elaborate tea parties, these women enjoy extensive social networks, and are well informed of events in the city and beyond.[6] In contrast, a new professional class of Uygur women is employed in offices, schools, hospitals and restaurants. Typically, they are not veiled, although some might wear a hat or scarf on their way to work. Western-styled skirts and trousers, even jeans, are the norm. In between the Khoja elite and young professionals are the more conservative housewives, the vendors of goods in the markets and the peasant cultivators. Physically active women in these categories wear skirts that vary in length from the knees to the ankles, long blouses and jackets, as well as brightly coloured scarves. Older women, however, prefer shoulder-length veils of a heavy dark-brown material; this invariably has a central flap to facilitate eye-to-eye contact for essential bargaining in the markets. Many newly rich families also encourage their women to adopt the veil, especially after marriage.

There is little sexual segregation in the Kashgar workforce. Uygur men and women work side by side; increasingly, they work together with Han Chinese, who have come to live in Kashgar, especially since 1999 when the rail link from Urumqi was completed. In contrast, gender divisions tend to govern social life. When middle-class Uygur families dine out in a modern Kashgar restaurant, for instance, they will typically hire a private room; for important festivities and family occasions they will hire a restaurant or private hall. Both kinds of occasions require men and women to sit separately. A similar segregation is observed in religious life. Social life for Kashgar's Uygur population revolves around the key Islamic rituals: birth, male circumcision, marriage and death, as well as the two Id festivals of

Ramadan and Kurban. Men and boys regularly visit mosques, but usually not women, although it is generally women who maintain religion traditions within the home. In contrast to the female mullahs of the Hui Muslim community who preside over some of the mosques of central China, Kashgar has no mosques run by women.

Despite this constraint, the high-caste Khoja ladies of Kashgar are very cultured and knowledgeable, even in matters of Islamic law and customs. They have acquired this expertise as members of religious families or because of their close associations with the imams. Some of them are known as buwums, female religious specialists who are held in high regard and serve not only as readers and interpreters of the Koran but also as community leaders, a role that includes washing the bodies of the dead preparatory to funerals. Most Uygur children attend Uygur language schools, although a few also visit madrasas (religious seminaries) to learn Arabic or study the Koran.

Kashgar is essentially a city of merchants. Many Uygur traders spend long periods managing businesses in Urumqi and the far-flung cities of eastern China, as well as the capitals of the neighbouring 'istans'.[7] Wives often assume the role of business partner for their husbands while they are away, keeping accounts, looking after investments and recruiting labour to work in offices and restaurants owned by their husbands outside the Kashgar region. The population of the old city also includes artisans, especially metalworkers and makers of musical instruments, and women who embroider dresses, shawls and tablecloths. The renewed economic prosperity of Kashgar is evident in the upward mobility of younger people, some of whom manage to leave the city to study and work in Urumqi and further afield, sometimes even abroad.

Ordam Padishah desert shrine, 1928.

BELIEFS AND PRACTICES

The religious culture of Kashgar's Uygur population is dominated by Sunni Islam. Many Uygur Muslims are followers of mystical Sufi teachers who lived and preached in and around Kashgar. The tombs of such figures are popular places of pilgrimage, even when located at some distance from the city itself. Visitors treat tombs as holy places, covering graves of saints with coloured cloths and banners that honour the dead, as well as serving as markers of the various visitors. Natural features near tombs are also invested with sanctity, as may be seen in the coloured ribbons tied to the branches of sacred trees, registering the wishes of devotees.

A tree of this type, standing next to a natural spring, is found halfway up a hill near the town of Kashgaria, a hour's drive south of Kashgar. A flight of steps beside the tree ascends a hill to the tomb of Mahmud Kashgari, who has now attained the status of a saint among present-day Uygurs. That devout Uygurs wish to be buried in the presence of such a holy personality is confirmed by the extensive cemetery that is sited at the base of this hill. The site has particular potency because it overlooks the point on the horizon at which the Tienshan and Pamir mountains meet. This is perhaps one of the oasis's oldest sacred sites.

The form of Sunni Islam followed by Kashgar's Ugyur population incorporates aspects of the shamanistic and animistic religions that were current in the Tarim Basin in earlier times, reflecting influences from Mongolia and Tibet. The syncretic feature of Uygur religious beliefs is best illustrated in the practices associated with rural cemeteries. Located next to the roads running through the Kashgar Oasis, these burial grounds tell stories of a mixed religious heritage in which shamanism and animism mingle with Islam. Chickens are often sacrificed to honour the dead, and trees are decorated with ribbons tied by women praying for children. When a child is sick, a bakshi, or shaman, is called in to exorcise the evil spirit. While he sings and beats a drum, the parents mould a clay doll, into which the evil spirit is made to flee. The doll is then taken to the family graveyard and left there instead of the sick child, who then recovers. Such a practice harks back to the Turkic-Mongolian origins of the Uygurs, who have a long tradition of making shamanistic dolls. The bakshi also cures psychologically disturbed patients by combining shamanistic rites with Islamic verses. On such occasions there is much drum beating and turbulent dancing, while the shaman calls out the names of Muslim saints and recites the poems of Sufi mystics. In many urban and rural shrines one can see sheep horns carefully

Apa Khoja tomb, surrounded by graves, 1928.

placed at the entrance or on the tombs, a reminder of the survival of old nomadic beliefs about the potency of animal spirits, which had to be propitiated before the slaughter of animals for human consumption.

Religious syncretism among Kashgar Uygurs also manifests itself in acts of pilgrimage. Pious Muslims who cannot afford to travel to Mecca and Medina make visits instead to desert cemeteries; these visits are regarded as being the equivalent of performing the haj. An example is the site near Yopurghu, celebrated for its laddered tombs partly buried by the shifting sands of the encroaching Taklimakan desert, some 80 kilometres north-east of Kashgar.

This funerary site, known as Ahlunlughun Maziri (it is also a desert sanctuary), is dotted with hundreds of graves each marked by a ladder, scattered around a large mound. This mound is believed to be the grave of Aktuluq (Ahunluq), reputedly one of the first Islamic preachers in the Kashgar region. Other factors contribute to the importance of this Islamic pilgrimage site, including the historic battles fought between the Qarakhanids Sufi warriors and remnants of an earlier Buddhist society. Each laddered tomb consists of a small oblong chamber roofed with a curved vault constructed from sun-baked mud bricks. Placed in front is a wooden ladder, surrounded by tree branches thrust into the sand, decorated with colourful flags that flutter in the desert breeze: the waving flags are thought to drive away evil spirits that may haunt the dead. The ladders

have a practical purpose, since they serve as stretchers to transport the dead to their final resting place. But the ladders also have a symbolic meaning. After the funeral they are thrust vertically into the ground, pointing towards the sky, so as to connect the dead with the heavens. Such beliefs may be traced back to earlier Nestorian, Manichaean and Zoroastrian religions, all of which venerate the sky and air as symbols of everlasting life.

The sanctuary at Yopurghu is also of interest for the innumerable mummies that have been found in the shifting sands. Typically, bodies of the dead were placed in the branches of the gigantic, gnarled poplars that guard this desert site, where they were exposed to birds and insects. After having been reduced to skeletons, the bodies fell to the ground and were then covered by sand, thereby ensuring their preservation in the extreme temperatures of the desert. While such tree burials seem no longer to take place, devotees still visit these sites.

The Ahlunlughun Maziri at Yopurghu forms part of the Ordam-padishah system to the south-east of Kashgar. Innumerable sanctuaries and sites are scattered throughout the region and have fascinated foreign visitors since an early report by Major Bellew in 1874.[8] Amongst the tombs lies that of the grandson of Satuq Bughra Khan, the first Islamic ruler of Kashgar. Known as the 'lion', Sayid Ali Arslan Khan was killed by beheading in 1095, in one of the many wars with the Buddhist kings of the region (especially Jukta Rashid and Nukta Rashid). His life, like that of Jesus, began as an immaculate conception,

British Consulate, with orchard grove, 1915.

to Bibi Miryam, the daughter of Satuq Bughra Khan – another local story that provides evidence of the long influence of Christian ideas in western China. A popular shrine to Bibi Miryam still exists on the road to Beshkerem. Eventually, Islam asserted itself, only to find that the shifting sands gradually claimed the cities of Lob and Katak from the middle of the fourteenth century onwards. Local legend says that dramatic sandstorms drowned the inhabitants in the salty sands as punishment for straying from Islam.

Another aspect of the syncretic religious system of Kashgar's Uygur population is the belief in mystical visions, as seen at a shrine containing seven masonry tombs in a small cemetery near the village of Opal, on the road towards Mahmud Kashgari's tomb. The local family that acts as guardian of this shrine claims that the tombs are those of seven Muslim saints. They explain that no actual bodies are buried here; rather, these saintly figures appeared to their grandfather in a dream. To mark this auspicious sign, their forefathers built the tomb, which now functions as a popular shrine. Local people offer wood, cloth and oil for lamps, with which to fashion the large incense sticks that are continuously burnt here. Each of the tombs is decorated with ram's horns, another reminder of the links between the Uygur and their older nomadic beliefs.

URBANISM AND MODERNIZATION

Kashgar today is a hybrid city, the old and the new standing in stark contrast to each other, yet despite this there is a growing respect for traditional solutions to familiar problems. Traditional Uygur medicine, for example, continues to thrive and the high value accorded to the wild red berries of Xinjiang has not been eroded. It is said that the Uygur have the highest longevity of all peoples, largely because of their diet and medical knowledge.

But the more visible signs of modernization suggest that many of the old ways have been destroyed. The modernization of Kashgar can be dated from about 1976, when the 8-kilometre road that connects Kashgar city to the airport was converted from a gravel track into a modern roadway. As other roads have been upgraded, the convenience of all-weather access has been counterbalanced by motorized vehicles replacing the charming traditional two-wheeled donkey carts called araba resinka (carts with rubber wheels). Country roads are still dominated by these typically overladen carts, but city and highway traffic has been taken over by trucks, jeeps, buses and cars. The result of technological change is that the relationship between animal power and mechanical power has changed. The famous giant donkeys of Yopurghu are now very expensive – one donkey costs about the same as two small cars, and yet is not as efficient as a modern automobile or a small truck.

The old walls of Kashgar have been progressively demolished and in the process the remains of the famous Swedish mission have totally disappeared. The Russian and British consulate buildings have, however, survived and can be located at the back of two modern, multi-storeyed hotels: the Semen and Chini Bagh respectively, both located on the ring road. New hotels, apartment blocks and roads have also led to the destruction of the last remaining 'tims' or Chinese watch towers in Kashgar. Many modern apartments in Kashgar are squashed against the remains of the old city walls; the citizens themselves often demand their demolition, saying that they constitute a safety risk, as they might collapse and fall on lower buildings and children who like to play in the shadow of the walls' remnants.

Industrialization came to Kashgar after the revolution of 1949. In particular, textile and carpet factories were set up using locally produced cotton and machinery imported from the cities on the eastern coast. Ancillary industries also developed, notably dyeing and cement production. Nearby Yecheng country produces large quantities of crude oil.

In strong contrast to these industrial activities are the extensive orchards of Kashgar, the defining character of this oasis town for so many centuries. Today, the village of Beshkerem supplies the city with a vast variety of melons, stone fruits and grapes. The grapes are grown on spectacular trellises that hang over the main roads that link the village to Kashgar city some 15 kilometres away. During the autumn the vines are stripped of leaves and rolled into balls, which are then dug into the earth. In this way the vines are protected from the winter cold and frost damage. In the spring, the vines are unfurled and trained up the trellises to again provide grapes and much-needed shade to human commuters, who constantly move back and forth between Kashgar city and its neighbouring villages.

TOURISM

Kashgar receives many overland visitors and traders from Central Asia, the Middle East, Russia and Pakistan. Typically they come for short periods to buy specific items at the famous Sunday Market and then make their way further inland to Turfan and neighbouring states. The Italians and French are the most prominent international tourists, but even they stay for only a day or two. Yet the remarkable attractions of Kashgar and its environs would justify a stay of at least a week. Tourism, however, depends on making the unique sites of the Kashgar region known to a wider audience – one of the objectives of this photographic essay.

The Old City of Kashgar remains unappreciated by visitors, yet it is an extraordinary example of a living, Islamic urban centre. The photographs in this book provide an insight into the visual beauty and tranquillity of the old city. Walking into the old city of Kashgar is something that all visitors should consider doing, in order to appreciate the unique Uygur architecture of the houses and street mosques[9] and to meet the residents, local vendors and artisans. Beyond the Kashgar prefecture, visitors can readily make their way northwards towards Urumuqi, the capital of Xinjiang, visiting amongst other sites the fabulous Buddhist caves of Kuche. They can also travel eastwards towards Khotan and other sites famed for their Buddhist relics. And while touring the Kashgar prefecture, modern-day visitors can read the quotations on page 153 to see what travellers in the past have said about this Old Silk Road city, its culture and people.

Woman flinging mud at a Sufi shrine as a cure for skin disease, 1915.

BETWEEN THE MOUNTAINS AND THE DESERT

Kashgar's sustained economic and cultural importance through the centuries is best understood from its favoured situation, at the heart of a well-watered oasis wedged between scorched wastelands and formidable mountains. To the east of the oasis is the dreaded Taklimakan Desert in the middle of the Tarim Basin, dipping in at least one place to more than 150 metres below sea level. The desert experiences minimal rainfall and extreme temperatures in summer and winter; humidity is virtually zero, with the result that nothing can grow here without irrigation. Traces of abandoned settlements and graveyards at the edges of the Taklimakan going back more than three thousand years indicate, however, that the climate was once less severe; perhaps in times past there was a greater density of population than there is today. An even more drastic limit to human settlement is provided by the mountains that ring the Kashgar Oasis on the other three sides. Rising abruptly to more than 5,000 metres above the floor of the oasis are the jagged peaks of the Tienshen to the north, the Pamirs to the west, and the parallel ranges of the Kunlun and Karakoram to the south, the last being crowned by K2, the highest mountain in the world after Everest. Many of the lower-lying mountains are rich in minerals; the reflected light from the copper inside the lower-lying ranges on the outskirts of Kashgar is blinding.

As the history of Kashgar illustrates, such daunting natural obstacles and climatic extremities were never an impediment to commercial and cultural contacts with the Chinese heartland to the east of the Taklimakan, or with the countries of Central Asia and South Asia that lay on the other side of the peaks – present-day Kyrgyzstan, Tajikistan, Uzbekistan and Pakistan. Today, as in the past, roads wind through mountain passes, some more than 4,000 metres high. That these arduous, summer-season routes were always a viable means of travel is abundantly illustrated in the long-standing narrative of the Old Silk Road, the southern routes of which passed through the Kashgar Oasis. Having been dormant for some time, because of the isolation of China from the rest of Asia, these thoroughfares are now once again active. Traffic is rapidly increasing on the recently refurbished Karakoram Highway, which connects Xinjiang with Pakistan, as well as on the new railway line that skirts the northern perimeter of the Taklimakan, linking Kashgar to Urumqi and other centres of Xinjiang and, beyond, to the cities

of central China. A new railway is planned between Kashgar and Hotan. These road and rail links are now being supplemented by air routes, and in 2007 it became possible for persons carrying EU passports to fly directly to Urumuqi and obtain their visas on arrival.

Seasonal streams from the surrounding mountains feed the Kashgar Oasis, permitting the cultivation that is crucial to provisioning Kashgar and its surrounding towns and villages, the total population of which now exceeds some 3.5 million people. The streams fan out into the oasis, but before they disappear without trace into the desert they are often directed into water channels that run beside roads. Because of the flat landscape of the oasis these roads are laid out in more or less grid-like formation. The characteristic vista of the oasis is, in fact, one of long straight roads extending to the horizon, lined for most of their length by tall elegant poplars – the characteristic trees of Central Asia. At either side of the roads stretches the arid and salty countryside, but when irrigated this is converted into fields of cotton, wheat and maize, as well as orchards of apples, plums, melons, pomegranates and the other fruits for which the Kashgar Oasis is famous. The delicious fruits of Kashgar have been noted by all visitors: in 1900, for instance, after Aurel Stein descended the Karakoram and was within easy distance of Kashgar he ate some apples and plums and wrote in his diary that this was 'the first fruit I had tasted for months'.

Beside the roads, and sometimes even across their intersections, are the elaborate wooden trellises for grapes. These are harvested only after they have been sun dried, contributing valuable crops of sultanas to the overall produce of the oasis. One recurring problem of the oasis is that the accelerating process of irrigation is taking its toll on the countryside, increasing areas of which have been rendered unfit for cultivation by salinization and alkalisation; a telltale salty residue now coats large expanses of the landscape. Where the countryside is fit for cultivation it is tended mostly by hand, though whenever possible local peasants exploit the strength of the mild-mannered, double-humped Bactrian camel which is common in the Kashgar Oasis, as elsewhere in Central Asia. Tractors are seen only occasionally.

Flanking the roads are the houses of the numerous Uygur villages that dot the oasis, and which depend on the city of

Kashgar for most of their livelihoods. Shut off from the outside by high, mud-clad walls, the houses are reached by wooden planks that traverse water channels next to the roads. Wooden doors, sometimes elaborately carved, give access to spacious courtyards surrounded by stables, stores and workshops. The family dwelling is usually positioned to the rear.

Uygur villages typically also house the local mosque and attached cemetery. In Xinjiang, residential dwellings are built right up to the mosque and tombs. In contrast to Christian thought, which is obsessed with evil spirits and ghosts that haunt the resting places of the dead, Islam in Xinjiang takes on a much more humanistic aspect. If a traveller has nowhere to stay, it is perfectly acceptable to sleep amongst the tombs. Local superstition takes on a nurturing aspect. All travellers, including truck drivers, carry copious volumes of nan, the local, rounded bread. This is no longer essential just for daily provisioning: travellers typically eat at wayside inns, but the ubiquitous nan is visibly displayed on the dashboard, for a barren dashboard is a dangerous omen.

The domineering Taklimakan Desert, China's largest desert and the second largest in the world after the Sahara, is an inhospitable wasteland, and yet it has a terrifying presence that

Snow clad peaks of the Tienshan range.

Mineral rich slopes on the outskirts of the Kashgar Oasis.

affects the lives of all the people who live on the rim of the Tarim Basin. The shifting sand dunes, which cover some 337,600 square kilometres, rise to between 3 and 6 metres but peter out as the desert meets the fringes of the oases. Sometimes a stony wasteland replaces the desert sands, as is the case with the landscape from Kashgar to Yarkand through which the southernmost part of the Old Silk Road passes. 'Taklimakan' is widely believed to mean 'place of no return', although new evidence suggests it actually means 'land of the poplar trees', poplars being a common feature of the outer ridge of the desert. The physical power of the desert is felt in the inner hearts of the oasis towns by the frequent sandstorms that well up with minimal warning, reduce visibility to a few metres and sometimes hold up normal life for two to three days at a time. Cancelled domestic flights are a common occurrence. At a more personal level, the desert has been experienced by many travellers with fear and trepidation: Hsuan-tsang, the seventh-century Chinese pilgrim who crossed the Taklimakan, spoke of being pursued by 'armies of demons'.

Though virtually no one can live here, the desert provides an ideal habitat for the dead, judging from a number of cemeteries for Kashgar Uygurs. Partly concealed by the shifting sands, some of these cemeteries are 'guarded' by gigantic poplar trees with characteristic gnarled trunks and branches. The diversiform-leaved poplar tree, different from the poplars that line the streets of Kashgar's villages, is said to live for a thousand years and resists collapse and decay for even longer. It is the ultimate symbol of life in the cemeteries of Kashgar. The most famous of the burial grounds in the Kashgar Oasis lies outside the village of Yopurghur, some 80 kilometres north-east of Kashgar. The funerary site of Ahunlughum Maziri is of particular interest for the hundreds of tombs sheltered by poplars. The graves are distributed around a large mound, identified with the burial place of the first Islamic preacher in the Kashgar region – this is not the only burial site attributed to him. Hollowed-out poplar trees form popular coffins, while flattened poplar strips are often found at burial sites, carrying written messages describing the physical features of the dead. As the desert proper asserts itself, the desert poplars become sparse, increasingly replaced by dying poplars and eventually only the drifting sands.

Kashgar is the largest oasis city of China, but it is not the only oasis. The second most important oasis is that of Yarkand, fed by the Yarkand River, which wends its way down from the Kunlun mountains. For centuries, Yarkand was the primary town of the Kashgar region because of its lucrative trade with India. Today, the vibrancy of Yarkand depends on the products of the oasis, the tombs of the Yarkand kings and the 'Twelve Muqam', the epic folk songs of the Uygur. The tomb of Aman-nisa Khan, the wife of the king who ruled Yarkand from 1553 to 1560, still stands. She is known as the poet-musician queen who collated the 'Twelve Muqam' into an organized sequence. Today Yarkand has traded its cultural importance for its former entrepôt function, allowing Kashgar to assert a permanent dominance in the region because of its railway link to Urumuqi.

The rugged lower hills and eroded slopes of the Tienshan range near Kashgar; from here rivers descend into the plain, feeding the subterranean water that sustains the oasis (above and right).

Flowering almond trees growing in an orchard near irrigated fields (left);
a lane running between the mud brick walls of village houses (below).

OVER PAGE A typical dirt lane lined with poplars, next to which water channels
run, in one of the many small villages of the Kashgar Oasis.

Beehive-shaped graves built of sun dried mud bricks in a rural cemetery on the road to Beshkerem (above);
local workmen clearing a nearby road (opposite).

Horses and donkeys are traditional modes of transport in the Kashar Oasis. The stronger, double-humped Bactrian camel (right above) is generally used for ploughing fields.

Trellises of poplar timbers are for training vines to produce raisins (left);
villagers digging irrigation canals with hoes (below).

OVER PAGE Trellises for vines meet over a road intersection near Beshkerem,
creating a shady spot that will eventually be completely covered by grapes.

Ancient desert poplar trees are sometimes treated as holy shrines, being clad in votive ribbons (left).
Other ancient desert poplar trees have partly collapsed (below), or are now engulfed by sand dunes (right).

Mud-brick graves and abandoned bones and skulls are clustered around ancient desert poplar trees near the tomb of a Sufi saint known as Aktuluq, in the dunes near Yopurghu.

OVER PAGE Densely packed rows of mud-brick graves, many with wooden ladders in front, populate the desert near Yopurghu; ancient poplars are seen in the distance.

Wooden ladders of mud-brick caves near Yopurghu are used for transporting corpses to the cemetery; the ladders are believed to symbolically link the deceased with heaven (above and right).

MERCHANTS AND MARKETS

Kashgar, the 'pivot' of Central Asia, has been above all else one of the largest international markets ever to dominate trade routes for so many centuries. Strategically located at the meeting point of the principal routes of the Old Silk Road, the life of Kashgar has always been determined by the movement of peoples, goods, cultures and religions.

Today, as in the previous thousand years, its markets attract traders from central China, as well as from neighbouring countries to the west and south. The commercial life of the Kashgar Oasis extends back to even earlier times, but those centres that were once bustling with merchants in the early centuries of the Christian era have now vanished, leaving only vestiges of decaying Buddhist monuments. While Kashgar is still appreciated throughout Xinjiang and the entire Central Asian region for its abundant agricultural produce, especially cotton, wheat, maize and sultanas, as well as locally woven cloths and caps, and finely crafted knives and metal wares, the city's true wealth depends on trade. Functioning as a land-bound entrepôt, Kashgar's markets are famous for the valuable goods imported from outside the Tarim Basin, such as finely woven silks from central and eastern China, carpets from Afghanistan and Turkmenistan and the skins from Central Asia. As in the past, foreign merchants make regular visits to the city; at the same time Kashgar's own traders travel to the far-away cities of the Chinese heartland and outside to establish lucrative businesses. This pattern of inter-regional networking is now much facilitated by the recently improved road, rail and air communications. The Chinese government's new policies to promote cross-border trade have also helped, in particular the rejuvenation of border crossings such as the Tuogart Pass.

The principal market of Kashgar was originally located in the square in front of the Idkah Mosque in the middle of the old city. As observed by European travellers, on Thursdays, or market days, it was congested with visitors, some mounted on donkeys and horses, as well as by caravans of camels and horses which bore great bales of cotton and other goods. In the summer the stalls were piled high with fruits, including peaches, apricots, mulberries, grapes, figs and melons of many varieties. Velvet and felt caps were a speciality, especially those embroidered with coloured and silver threads or trimmed with fur. In the side streets were located the bazaars of the blacksmiths and silversmiths, and the sellers of flour and other grains; numerous partridges were displayed in cages.

This market was partly displaced when a new avenue was cut through the middle of the old city. Even so, the Idkah Mosque still maintains its long-standing links with urban commercial activities. Shops selling copper and brass wares, as well as stalls offering tea, breads and skewered meats, cluster around three sides of the compound walls of the mosque; one entire section is reserved for locally made musical instruments, another for wooden furniture and metallic boxes. There are even second-hand clothing stalls, and old-fashioned apothecaries offering Chinese and Uygur remedies. As for the square itself, this has been cleared of stalls and now functions mainly as a site of recreation, with young men of Kashgar playing billiards. Cut off from the mosque, in the narrow lanes on the other side of the new avenue, is the main food and spice market of the city, as well as stalls selling a full range of felt and velvet caps, including those from neighbouring Tajikistan and Kyrgyzstan.

Outside the old city, on the opposite bank of the Tuman River, is the present-day Sunday Market for which Kashgar is famous. Once occupying an outdoor space, the market is now partly accommodated in a vast, purpose-built concrete building. In spite of this somewhat unsympathetic setting, it is crowded with merchants selling a huge variety of produce and wares: grains, vegetables, fruits, meat and eggs; household furniture and utensils, knives and farming equipment; embroidered caps and cloths; imported spices, carpets, silks and animal skins. A short distance away, near the riverbank, are the open grounds where traders deal in horses, camels, mules, goats and chickens. The roads all around are jammed with vehicles and animal-drawn carts, and there is an unmistakable festive atmosphere.

An idea of how Kashgar's Sunday Market must have appeared in times past may be had from a similar, but smaller market in the provincial town of Yengisar, some 50 kilometres south-east of Kashgar. Here everyone travels to market on foot or on carts drawn by horses, mules and even camels. Agricultural produce, equipment and animals are a speciality, since this market caters particularly to the rural population of the Kashgar Oasis. Temporary stalls with cloth canopies are set up beside the streets outside the town. Here shoppers from the surrounding villages refresh themselves with tea and freshly cooked, mutton-filled pastries known as samsa; video entertainment is also on offer. While the volume of goods and animals for sale in Yengisar may be less than that of Kashgar's Sunday Market, there is no lack of people or commercial activity.

In observing the markets of Kashgar, Yengisar and Yarkand today we should remember that it was the fame of Uygur traders that first brought the English into Xinjiang. The first European description we possess of the Uygur merchants comes from Robert Shaw, a British tea planter, who visited southern Xinjiang in 1868. He called the Uygurs 'Torkees' and 'Mughals', and first encountered them in Leh, in modern-day Ladakh. Then, as now, Uygur merchants from Kashgar were spread out well beyond the boundaries of the Kashgar oasis:

> *Their large white turbans, their beards, their long and ample outer robes, reaching nearly to the ground, and open in front showing a shorter under-coat girt at the waist, their heavy riding boots of black leather, all gave them an imposing aire; while their dignified manners, so respectful to others, and yet so free from Indian cringing or Tibetan buffoonery, made them seem like men amongst monkeys compared with the people around them.*
> (Shaw 1871, p. 11)

On 9 December 1868 Shaw became the first English person to walk through the gates of Yarkand; he rapidly moved on to Yengisar and then Kashgar, where he spent some three months as the prisoner of Yaqub Beg. Shaw had a special interest in pack animals: he observed that no mules were bred in the Kashgar region because the horse was regarded as pure (halal) and the donkey as impure (haram). Even today, mules are regarded as an insult to God – being the product of human husbandry, the mule is seen as yet another attempt by man to compete with the creator. Today, Kashgar remains devoid of mules but instead is famous for its giant black donkeys, which are the size of small horses.

Crowds of shoppers on their way to the Sunday Market.

Double-humped camels and small horses are both used for pulling carts laden with goods to markets in the Kashgar Oasis.

Animals have always played a major part in the diet, economy and trade of the Kashgar oasis. The favourite food of the Uygurs is pullao, a baked rice dish cooked with mutton or chicken, carrots, onions and spices. The Sunday Market is also a festive occasion in which to indulge in various Uygur delicacies, including mutton stews and meat dumplings washed down with fresh pomegranate juice. Animal parts also play an important role in traditional medicine and religious rites; it is common to see animal horns in apothecaries and cemeteries, possibly as symbols of physical strength and endurance.

It has been said that the Sunday Market of Kashgar attracts no fewer than 100,000 traders, big and small, rich and poor – many poor peasant women stand with their fragile eggs next to the large horse traders. Kashgar used to be famous for its 'sleeve trading'; the merchants wore jackets with oversized sleeves in which they could hide their hands. Sellers never called out their prices, preferring to press and pull the knuckles and fingertips of the buyer in an age-old code that ruled the bidding wars between competing merchants. Today, sleeve trading has largely died out, but it continues in the animal markets of the Kashgar region, although increasingly it is viewed with resentment because it said to promote dishonesty and cheating.

Crowds of both men and women enthusiastically shopping for clothes imported from other parts of China and locally grown vegetables at the Sunday Market.

Women examine lengths of cloth at the Sunday Market (left), but the main bazaar for men's hats is in the narrow lane running beside the Idkah Mosque (above).

Bolts of gorgeously brocaded silk cloths on sale in a store at the Sunday Market (above) and a jacket from the same cloth worn proudly by a woman shopper (right).

Donkeys still hitched to their carts resting beside the river near the Sunday Market (above),
while men inspect cows in the animal section of the market (left).

Guarded by villagers
and roped together in
bunches are these
sheep being sold at the
Sunday Market.

A common practice at the Sunday Market is 'sleeve trading', by which prices are agreed upon by squeezing and pulling fingers and knuckles; only then is money exchanged.

The Sunday Market is a convenient time for men to have their heads massaged and their beards shaved, both by junior apprentices and experienced practitioners.

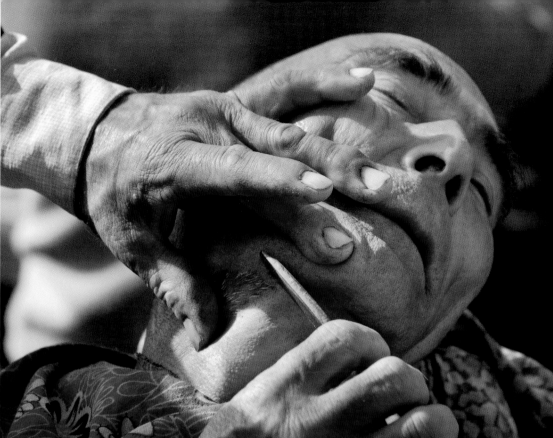

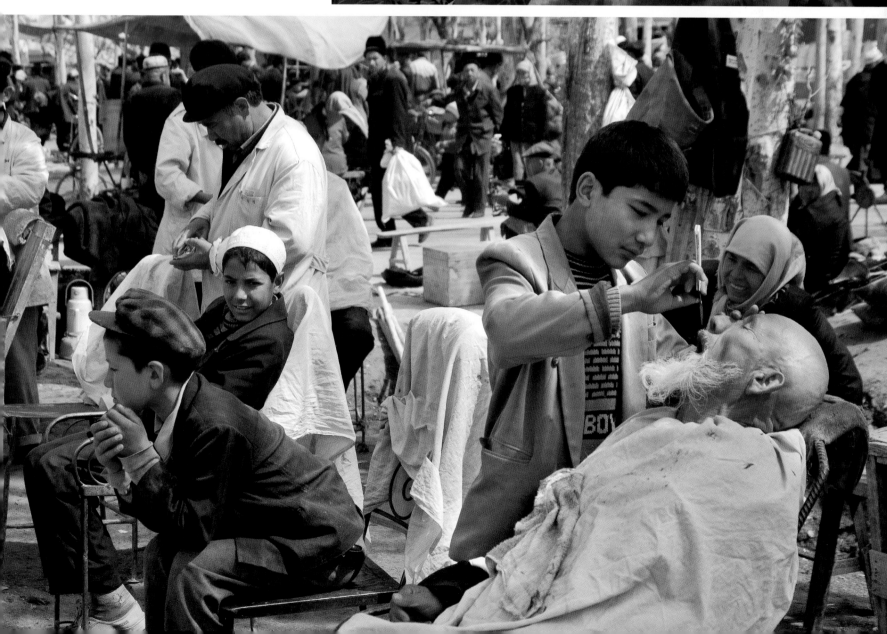

Tall, cylindrical woollen caps typical of the Kashgar region are worn with dignity by both men and women at the Sunday Market.

Elderly men at the Sunday Market wear a range of fur-trimmed caps, woollen caps and embroidered caps, all of local manufacture.

Cutting and dicing lamp for making the dumplings called samsas (left); these delicacies are eaten in the stalls frequented by men at the Sunday Market (below).

Samsas are cooked by steaming or baking before being served piping hot.

Sheep intestines are considered a great delicacy (left), but breads of all types are an everyday necessity (above).

OVER PAGE A stall displaying spices, nuts and dried fruits in the daily market in Kashgar's Old City.

Villagers beside the roads on the outskirts of Kashgar sell home grown gourds (below) and garlands of freshly picked garlic (right).

Artisans in the Old City fashion brass objects or repair old shoes (left); meanwhile a vendor with his metal wash basins awaits customers beside an outlying road (below).

THE OLD CITY

Kashgar is the best-preserved example of a traditional Islamic city to be found anywhere in Central Asia. Occupying a mound overlooking a bend in the Tuman River, a run-off from the nearby Tienshen mountains, the Old City consists of a labyrinth of tightly interlocking streets and lanes, originally protected by a circuit of walls created of rammed earth. Where fully preserved, these walls are about 8 metres thick and up to 10 metres high, reinforced by regularly placed, circular buttresses. They define an approximately elliptical zone, extending a little more than 1,000 metres from east to west and about 600 metres from north to south. Dating back to the seventeenth and eighteenth centuries, when Kashgar came under the sway of the Khoja khans, the walls survive today only in limited stretches, as on the northern side of the city. However, early European visitors to Kashgar commented on their crenellations as well as their massive iron gates, which were shut at sunset and opened at daybreak, to the blowing of horns and firing of guns. Nothing now remains of the arched entryways that led to the gates that protected Kashgar's citizens in times of trouble. Better preserved are the ramparts defining the part-circular 'citadel' on the western flank of Kashgar. Probably here were located the palaces of the Khojas, but they have long ago been replaced by the municipal police headquarters.

Like the gates of the Old City, the broad moat that ran around the walls has also fallen victim to the development that has overtaken Kashgar since the 1980s, when the ring road encircling the old city was laid out. It was at about the same time that a broad avenue was cut ruthlessly through the crowded lanes and houses, though sparing the Idkah Mosque, the principal place of worship in the middle of the Old City.

In spite of these modernising interventions, the traditional urban quality of Kashgar has by no means been obliterated: barely a few metres away from the ring road and the broad avenue that bisects the Old City lies a world that harks back to another era. Here densely packed houses linked by streets and lanes wind in an apparently haphazard fashion from one end of the walled city to the other. To early European visitors these thoroughfares were narrow and dirty, and mostly muddied from the water that slopped over from pails carried by donkeys and humans. The lack of modern piping means that these means of transporting water may still be seen in some quarters. Donkeys pulling carts are the most common means of transport, though small motorized vehicles are becoming popular. Refreshment is on offer throughout the Old City, judging from the numerous and well-patronized tea shops, or chai khanas.

An unusual feature of the Old City is the pavement that distinguishes thoroughfares from dead-end lanes: wider streets, lined with hexagonal slabs, originally stone pieces but now mostly replaced by concrete, are used by wheeled traffic and animals, while narrow lanes, generally no wider than 2 metres and paved with brick surfaces, invariably end in clusters of houses. Whether wide or narrow, these streets and lanes are for the most part hemmed in by high, mud-clad walls, behind which lie the residences of Kashgar's population. The walls are broken by wooden doors with ornately carved frames, and often overlooked at an upper level by shuttered windows and occasional balconies. At many places the rooms of these dwellings project over the street. Sometimes they extend all the way across the streets to create dark, tunnel-like passages. Whether open to the sky or roofed by timbers carrying the floors of rooms above, the streets and lanes serve as important thoroughfares, linking the central square of the Idkah Mosque where the principal markets are located to the outer walls of the city. The intersections of these thoroughfares are sometimes punctuated by lesser mosques and madrasas, which serve as neighbourhood places of prayer.

The houses of Kashgar's Old City are invariably of the courtyard type, whether they are large mansions belonging to rich merchants or more modest dwellings of artisans and labourers. Rooms are generally arranged on two or more levels around an open, paved space that is planted with the fig trees and rose bushes that are much loved by Kashgar's citizens. Carved out of poplar, the ubiquitous tree of the Kashgar Oasis, are slender wooden columns with ornate brackets carrying the rafters of the ceilings, and the balconies that run around the upper rooms, overlooking a courtyard below.

Rooms at the lower level are used as reception and dining areas, generally known as mihman khanas; their wooden floors are covered with carpets and bolsters, with additional coverings stored in wall cupboards with ornate doors. In the houses of the wealthier citizens, such rooms are further enhanced by colourful curtains and glass chandeliers. Sometimes there is an additional sitting area for the men, called a supa/sopa, on one side of the courtyard, near the entrance from the street. The kitchen is usually consigned to one corner of the courtyard, and is far from spacious. An exterior flight of narrow wooden steps gives access to an upper balcony, off which open the private rooms of the house, reserved for the women and children of the household, and used for sleeping. The steps generally continue to a rooftop terrace, where more often than not there is a pigeon cage created from a timber framework covered in wire. It is these coops that give the Old City its distinctive jagged skyline. The birds are mostly bred for eating, grilled pigeon being one of the culinary delicacies of Kashgar.

Though traditional in the houses of Kashgar's Old City, this lower/upper and male/female division is by no means always enforced. In a grand mansion owned by the wealthiest cotton dealer of some hundred years ago and still inhabited by his descendants, for instance, the rooms at the ground level are used as offices and shops, while the formal reception area with a built-in fireplace – surely a luxury in those days – is relegated to the upper level. The house is of interest for the wooden panels fashioned as arched profiles 'suspended' between the columns of the courtyard at both lower and upper levels. This feature is common in most of the larger dwellings with upper balconies that survey the traffic of principal streets of the Old City. Their imposing façades, with balconies topped with 'suspended' arched panels, testify to the commercial significance of Kashgar in the nineteenth and early twentieth centuries. Today these wooden atrium houses are distinguished in some cases by yellow plaques hammered above the ornately carved doorways; these are municipal notices declaring the family members of that house to be 'model citizens of Kashgar'.

Newly built offices, stores and apartments line the ring road, which marks the original circuit of walls that once surrounded the Old City. Here many of Kashgar's Uygur citizens have now shifted, preferring the amenities of a modern concrete dwelling with parking facilities to a wooden courtyard house. Tucked away behind these high-rise developments are occasional vestiges of the past, including the British and Russian Consulates. As residences of European emissaries to what was then known as Chinese Turkestan they are built in an obviously European style, and were once surrounded by spacious shady gardens and orchards. While their grounds have fallen victim to unbridled development, both the British and Russian Consulates still stand. Admittedly, the former survives only as a banquet hall attached to a modern hotel known today as Chini Bagh, or Chinese Garden, imitating the original name of the embassy.

Here, too, are located the cemeteries, not only of the Europeans but also of the Uygur Muslim and Chinese communities.

Access to the Old City sometimes takes the form of a gentle walk into the tight lanes that characterize the town; at other times access requires the ascent of steep steps of some hundred metres, depending on which side of the mound one tackles. Within the precincts of the old city are some forty mosques, ornately decorated in traditional Uygur style; and one old well reputedly dates from the days of Yaqub Beg. Intruding on the tranquillity of the houses and artisan quarters are the noisy motorbikes of Kashgar's youth, who fancy themselves as members of a much faster, modern way of life. The modern motorbike and the traditional donkey increasingly vie for space on the narrow lanes.

Portions of the massive mud brick walls that once completely encircled the Old City (below, opposite and over page).

Entrance to one of the covered lanes (left), and inside a covered lane (right), both paved with square bricks.

OVER PAGE Poplar beams supporting the upper rooms of a dwelling provide shade to a passage paved with hexagonal bricks.

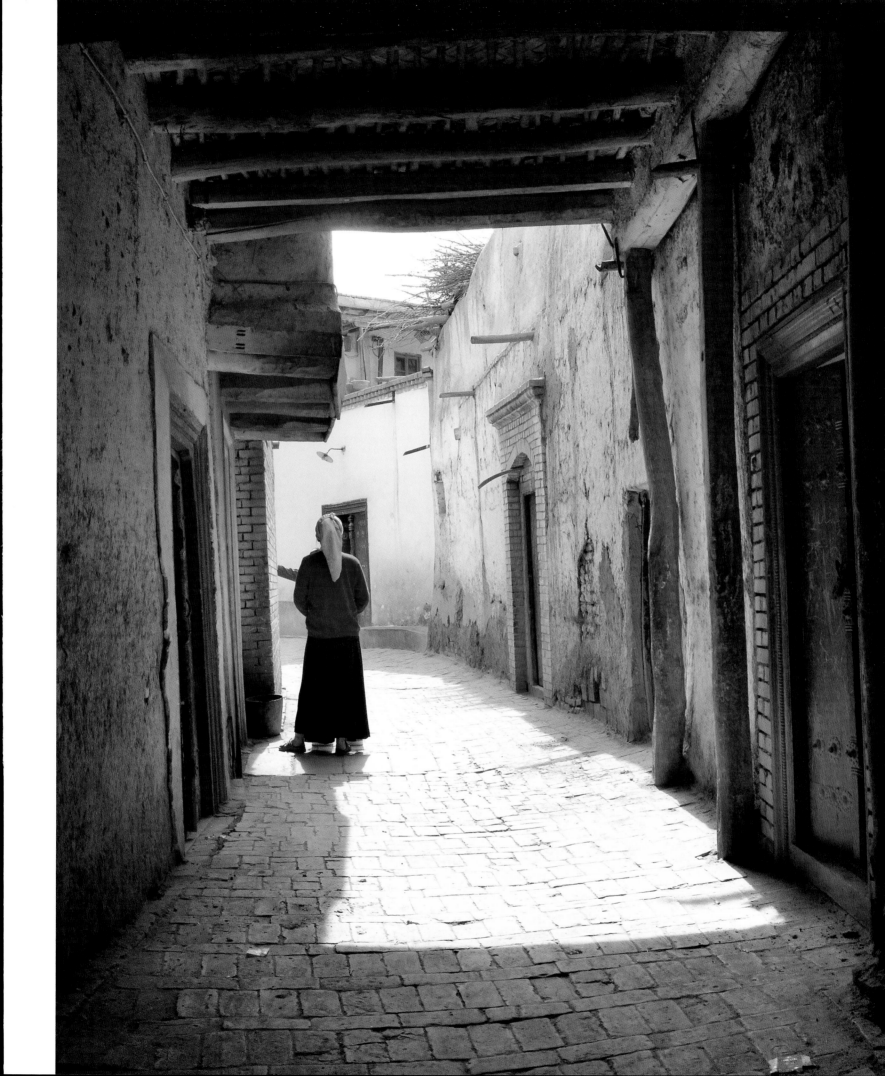

Kashgar's inhabitants enjoying a rare shaded spot (left), making their way along a curved lane (below), or carefully descending a steep flight of steps (opposite).

Shopping in the narrow lanes is facilitated by vendors with bicycle carts selling fruits and vegetables.

OVER PAGE Shops and stalls are located in the wider streets suitable for animal carts.

Some of the activities in the Old City. Children boxing (left) and women washing at a communal tap (above).

OVER PAGE Panorama across the Old City, showing the flat, mud-clad roofs of houses, many topped with pigeon coops.

One dwelling has an outer courtyard entered directly from a lane (left above), while another has a double-storeyed courtyard (below left).Living quarters and kitchens are typically cluttered (below).

Larger houses have flights of steps climbing up to arcaded balconies (left), in other such dwellings, balconies look down on glazed-in courtyards (above).

This wealthy merchant's house has a spacious carpeted verandah (left and right). The main reception room is decked with bright carpets and curtains (below right).

OVER PAGE The carpeted reception room in another merchant's house has richly plastered wall niches to display textiles and household goods.

Multi-storeyed buildings with dwellings over shops are distinguished by arcaded balconies with curious 'suspended' arches that over-look the main commercial streets.

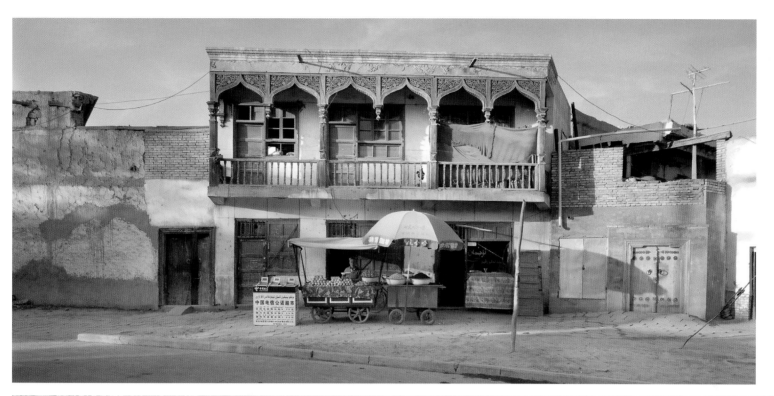

The Russian Consulate is built in a distinct European style (left), and contrasts with the British Consulate, which has a traditional wooden verandah (below left) and a newly restored, richly plastered interior (right).

MOSQUES AND SHRINES

The focus of Kashgar's Old City is a great congregational place of prayer known as the Idkah Mosque. Today this faces on to an open plaza, now a recreational site crowded with men playing snooker but in the past the site of Kashgar's principal market, the stalls of which are now consigned to the sides and rear of the walled compound. Dating back to the fifteenth century, the Idkah Mosque was substantially remodelled in 1838; it has been further restored in recent years. The mosque is entered from the east through a yellow-brick gateway flanked by a pair of tapering, squatly proportioned circular minarets, more than 10 metres high. The gateway gives access to a peaceful garden courtyard, planted with poplars lining a crossing of two pathways, beyond which is the prayer hall, some 160 metres long, where several hundreds of worshippers gather each Friday. Lines of slender wooden pillars support a flat roof. Its ceiling is divided into bays decorated with diverse geometric designs of Middle Eastern origin, as well as more characteristic Chinese floral motifs, all painted in vivid blues, greens, yellows and pinks. The central bays of the prayer hall are partly enclosed by masonry walls, since this part of the mosque is reserved for winter usage; a prayer niche is set into the back wall.

Lesser neighbourhood prayer halls are found throughout the city, many of them raised up above the level of the surrounding streets. Though smaller than the Idkah Mosque, they also have columned prayer halls, divided into open areas for the summer season and closed areas appropriate for winter. One of the finest is the Orda-ishki Mosque, built in 1875 by Yaqub Beg of Khoqand. The ornate plasterwork of the prominent prayer niche in its rear wall has now been refashioned. The nearby Khaluq Madrasa, dating back to the seventeenth century, consists of a rectangular courtyard surrounded by arcades with doorways leading to vaulted chambers, once used by theological students. The complex is now in a sadly incomplete condition.

Of equal religious significance are the saintly tombs, or mazars, built on the outskirts of Kashgar. The most important is the Apa Khoja complex, 5 kilometres north-east of the city. This is the burial place of the Khoja Khan, who died in 1694, and his various family members, all of whom were members of the Naqshbandi Sufi sect. Local people believe that the remains of the celebrated Ipar Han, the Kashgar-born 'Fragrant Concubine' of the Qing emperor, were buried here after she was carried back to Kashgar following her death in Beijing in 1788. The famous portrait of her by Giuseppe Castiglione known also as Lang Shining (c.1760), an Italian Jesuit priest at the emperor's court in Beijing, shows a young determined woman in battle gear. Legends say that the bier inside the mausoleum was the very one that carried her back to Kashgar. Recent historical evidence, however, suggests that Ipar Han was probably buried on a royal site on the outskirts of northern Beijing. In 1930 Gunnar Jarring reported powerful signs of the links between Islam and shamanism when he shot a now famous photograph showing the many Marco Polo sheep horns stacked at the entrance to the tomb.

Apa Khoja's mausoleum, the largest funerary structure in Xinjiang and a popular pilgrimage centre, comprises a cubical chamber topped by a dome more than 25 metres high. The outer walls of the tomb are enlivened by bright blue and white ceramic tiles, while green tiles clad the corner circular towers and dome. The building stands in the middle of an extensive walled cemetery, crowded with mud-brick domed graves. Among the subsidiary structures of the Apa Khoja complex is a madrasa, with a wooden columned hall and a masonry domed chamber. The complex also includes a mosque with an extensive prayer hall with carved wooden columns and brackets carrying a flat ceiling; the side wings consist of arcaded domed chambers. The ceiling panels over the central bays of the prayer hall have geometric designs as well as painted scenes of local landscapes. Both the prayer hall and side chamber open on to a garden courtyard planted with poplars. The complex is entered through an arched portal flanked by minaret-like towers topped by lanterns. The panel over the doorway has a calligraphic inscription composed of brilliant blue and white tiles.

On the southern perimeter of Kashgar is the Mazar of Yusup Has Hajip, an intellectual and poet who lived in Kashgar in the eleventh century. Virtually rebuilt in the 1980s, this complex consists of a masonry domed mausoleum standing in a walled compound, entered through a monumental arched portal. The tomb itself is entirely clad in blue and white tiles of recent manufacture which also extend on to the corner circular towers. A more authentic ancient tomb is the Arslan Mazar to the east of the city, reputedly housing the remains of an eleventh-century Qarakhanid ruler but unlikely to predate the fifteenth century.

Kashgar's Idkah Mosque, the largest in the city, is entered through an arched gateway flanked by minarets (below). Within the garden courtyard inside stands a small pavilion, from which sermons are sometimes given (right).

The cuboid brick structure, complete with dome, is devoid of any decoration, but the arched entryway on the south is topped with a geometric plaster screen.

The mazar of another figure of this dynasty is located at Etachi, just outside Artush, about 40 kilometres north of Kashgar. Supposedly the last resting place of Sutuq Bughra, the first Qarakhanid khan to be converted to Islam, the tomb is similarly cuboid in appearance, with a prominent frontal arched portal, all built in brick. Corner circular towers have domical lanterns picked out in deep blue tiles; similarly coloured tiles also clad the dome. 'Sutuq' means 'merchant', an apt name for this famous resident of the renowned commercial town of Artush.

About 55 kilometres south of Kashgar, near the village of Opal, is the mazar of Mahmud Kashgari. Returning from Baghdad to die in Kashgar in 1105, this celebrated literary figure has now attained the status of a saint, with the result that his tomb has become a pilgrimage destination. The mazar crowns the summit of a small hill with a distant view of the meeting of the Tienshan and Pamir ranges, considered to be a particularly sacred landscape. At the base of the flight of steps that ascends the hill are a natural spring and a tree draped in votive threads; on the other side of the hill stretches a vast cemetery. The walled compound in which the mahmud's tomb stands is entered through a cubical domed structure adorned with monochrome brickwork in relief patterns. The tomb itself is fronted by a line of carved and painted columns, between which are geometric wooden screens that admit light to the tomb chamber; in the middle is the mahmud's huge whitewashed plastered grave. The traditional type of flat-roofed, timber chamber contrasts with four lesser rear rooms of the complex, built of masonry and topped by domes.

Additional examples of Islamic architecture are to be found in and around the city of Yarkand. The oldest is the Azna Mosque, dating back to the fifteenth century and built in an obviously Middle Eastern manner. Entered through an imposing arched portal, the mosque consists of a courtyard with trees and a well, surrounded on all sides by arcades. In the middle of the west side is another arched portal. This gives access to the main prayer hall, roofed with a lofty brick dome.

Other mosques in Yarkand conform more to Central Asian schemes. They include the Jami Masjid in the middle of the city, which has a central enclosed area for winter prayer in the middle, flanked by open colonnades with slender wooden columns at either side. The mosque faces on to a royal cemetery. Apart from a somewhat incongruous modern wooden mausoleum of Sultan Saidhan, one of Yarkand's sixteenth-century khans, the cemetery is dotted with a number of tile-clad, domed tombs dating from the nineteenth century. Many of these are linked to the representatives of the Qing emperors who governed Yarkand at this time. The most popular of these funerary monuments is the Tomb of Seven Sultans. Somewhat severely plain externally, this building is of interest for seven large graves sheltered by a wooden ceiling. Another, much venerated saintly tomb is that of Khoja Muhammad Serip, tutor to Sultan Saidkhan of the kingdom of Yarkand. Here an entrance vestibule decorated with brightly toned murals leads to a chamber roofed with a lofty brick dome. This accommodates the grave of the saint, now almost totally obscured by a dense cluster of cloth banners.

The pillared prayer hall of the Idkah Mosque is divided into an enclosed winter chamber (below) and an open summer chamber (centre). One of the lesser mosques of the Old City has a minaret rising over the entrance gate (right).

The Mazar of Yusup Has Hajip, an 11th century literary figure, on the outskirts of Kashgar, is entirely clad in modern ceramic tiles (left); even the tomb within the whitewashed domed chamber is tiled (right and below).

Other funerary monuments on the fringes of Kashgar include the Arslan Mazar (left) and Ak Mazar below. The largest of these is the Apa Khoja Complex, entered through a tile-clad gate (right), beside which is small brick mosque (far right).

The tomb of Apa Khoja is clad in coloured tiles, its corner minarets soaring above the graves in the surrounding cemetery (left). The imposing domed interior is also crowded with graves, including that of the founder of the Khoja dynasty (above).

The prayer hall in the Apa Khoja Complex has a pillared interior covered in mats (above).
Masonry arches give access to a surrounding arcade, sometimes used as a madrasa, or theological
school (right).

124 KASHGAR

Wooden columns, brackets, beams and ceiling panels of the prayer hall in the Apa Khoja Complex are decorated with bright floral patterns, geometric designs and local landscape scenes (left and above).

OVER PAGE In the desert near the village of Opal on the fringe of the Kashgar Oasis is an extensive graveyard with a distant view of the Tienshan and Pamir ranges.

The Mazar of Mahmud Kashgari, the celebrated 11th century scholar, crowns the hill above Opal (below). The tomb stands within a walled enclosure, entered through an arched gateway topped by a dome and framed by slender finials (right).

The grave of Mahmud Kashgari is housed in a simple chamber with intricately worked, geometric wooden screens (left and below). Smaller and simpler funerary buildings, also with wooden screens, are found elsewhere in the Kashgar Oasis (right).

Royal tombs in the Kashgar Oasis include the newly restored Mazar of Sutuq Bughra Khan at Stachi, near Artush (left), and the newly built mausoleum of a poetess queen in the Altunluq Cemetery at Yarkand (right and below).

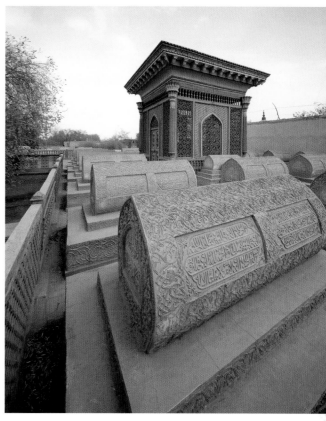

Graves in the Altunluq Cemetery at Yarkand (right) surround a dilapidated tomb with a tile covered dome (left). The mosque in the nearby Khoja Muhammad Serip Complex has a decorated prayer hall (bottom left) and a wooden calligraphic screen (below).

The tomb of Khoja Muhammad Serip is a modest domed structure, approached through a decaying porch (above). Interior domed chambers have graves adorned with clusters of poles (right), some with brightly coloured banners (left).

OVER PAGE The entrance chamber to the tomb is adorned with wall paintings, many with Persian inscriptions giving historical information and offering felicitations to the saint.

Other monuments in Yarkand include the Azna Mosque, entered through a tile-clad gateway (left), with a courtyard surrounded by arcaded chambers (below), as well as the tomb of Abdurahman Wang and his family members (right).

People come at any time to pray at saintly tombs, such as the Mazar of the Seven Sultans in the Altunluq Cemetery in Yarkand (left), or a small mausoleum near the Aslan Mazar in Kashgar (below).

Burial sites in the Kashgar Oasis are cluttered with offerings, such as rams' horns and water flasks, deposited by worshippers (above), or clay dolls moulded by parents wishing to help sick children being cured by shamans (right).

EXPLORING VESTIGES OF THE PAST

The oasis of Kashgar witnessed a rapid growth of human settlements from the beginning of the Christian era, when caravans loaded with merchandise travelled along the peripheries of the Taklimakan Desert. Trade along the Silk Road was inevitably accompanied by religious beliefs and practices, which explains how Buddhism came to spread rapidly from India permanently to China and, for a time, the Middle East. By the third century of the Christian era Buddhism in both its Hinayana and Mahayana forms was well established in the Tarim Basin.

Although Buddhism did not outlast the impact of Islam in later centuries, the Kashgar Oasis, like other parts of Xinjiang, is dotted with vestiges of the Buddhist period. These monasteries and sanctuaries were abandoned long ago, and survive today only in a decaying and dilapidated state. Even so, they were sufficiently visible to attract the attention of a growing number of European archaeologists, geographers, diplomats, missionaries and spies. This motley group of voyagers arrived in what was then known as Chinese Turkestan, either by making their way over the perilously high passes of the Karakoram mountains from British India, or by taking trains through the recently acquired Central Asian provinces of Russia and then wending their way through the ranges.

Among the diverse band of adventurers who arrived in Kashgar at the end of the nineteenth century and the early years of the twentieth were Sven Hedin, Marc Aurel Stein, Albert Van de Coq, Paul Pelliot and the exotically entitled Hungarian aristocrat Count Kozui Otani. Many of these figures stayed with the British Consul at Chini Bagh, the comfortable residence set in orchards on the outskirts of the old city of Kashgar that served as the headquarters of the British mission from the 1890s onwards. Aided by locally recruited helpers, these explorers fanned out into the Kashgar oasis, where they busied themselves with surveying, measuring, photographing and excavating the various Buddhist remains. In the process they gathered a rich harvest of archaeological observations and artefacts that supplemented the written accounts of the region's early history. These collections were of outstanding interest, since they provided the first material evidence of the merchandise, social customs and religious beliefs that were conveyed along the Old Silk Road in the early centuries of the Christian era. However, the enthusiasm of these European investigators for ancient artefacts also spawned a number of forgeries, which were not detected for many decades.

Lured by antiquities, either authentic or fake, these determined explorers kept detailed diaries that still make for entertaining reading; indeed their observations of everyday life in the Kashgar region and its surrounding towns, let alone the machinations of the Great Game, constitute a colourful historical record of the period. The ancient Buddhist monuments in the Tarim Basin which they documented are for the most part still to be seen, even if the explorers were responsible for removing to museums in India and Europe many of the cloth paintings and plaster sculptures, and even portions of the wall and ceiling paintings, that they discovered. Thanks to these findings, several sites have become world famous, none more so than the painted 'caves' dating from the fifth to seventh centuries at Dunhuang to the east of the Tarim Basin, and Kizil, about 800 kilometres north-east of Kashgar. Stein was particularly active in the area around Khotan, some 500 kilometres south-east of Kashgar, where he unearthed a large hoard of paper manuscripts and cloth paintings, many now housed in the British Museum.

Though the monuments in the vicinity of Kashgar oasis are less spectacular in appearance than those at Dunhuang and Kizil, they have an even longer ancestry, as they are amongst the earliest Buddhist sites in Central Asia. This reflects their location at the entry points into China from the southern section of the Old Silk Road that links Kashgar to India and Pakistan. Though sadly deteriorated, they nonetheless constitute significant evidence of the culture and religion that once dominated the Kashgar region.

The most imposing monument of the Kashgar oasis is Mauri Tim (locally known as the Mor Pagoda), about 30 kilometres north of Kashgar on the outskirts of the orchards of Beshkerem. First documented in 1900 by Stein, this site probably dates back to the first or second century, when the Tarim Basin was under the sway of the Kushanas – the Central Asian rulers of Turkic origin, who subsequently established themselves in what is now northern Pakistan and central India. Mauri Tim consists of a pair of brick stupas, or commemorative mounds, some 50 metres apart, arranged in an approximate north–south line. Raised on a natural eminence, and therefore exposed to the eroding effects of the severe desert winds, the stupas consist of solid hemispheres on square bases, constructed of sun-dried, mud

Distant view of the two stupas at Mauri Tim.

brick. The northern stupa is less decayed, and it is still possible to make out three diminishing square terraces, one superimposed upon the other. The dome-like superstructure is raised on a high cylindrical base, relieved by arched niches in the middle of four sides, no doubt intended to accommodate Buddhist sculptures but now empty. Only the sloping walls of the southern stupa's square base can now be made out. Eroded walls in the vicinity of Mauri Tim suggest an associated settlement, possibly a monastery for visiting Buddhist monks. Stein noted other nearby ruins, including a 'Pigeon House', a funerary structure that possibly housed the remains of Nestorian Christian burials (Stein 1904, p. 138). By 2005 this had disappeared entirely; local peasants had purchased the land back from the municipality and dug the remaining ruins into the soil.

Approximately 5 kilometres south-east of Mauri Tim, across a dried-up lake, is an extensive complex of dissolving mud-brick structures known today as Khan-oi. These were possibly the residences and palaces of a local line of rulers, most likely Buddhists, who had settled here in the fifth or sixth century, but this interpretation remains a mere hypothesis. The site is surrounded by massive walls, which indicate a citadel of some type, though no overall plan can be determined without surveying and excavation. Khan-oi, together with Topa Tim, a few kilometres to the north-east, were both noticed by Stein, but his explorations were in the nature of a preliminary report (Stein 1904, pp. 134–8). Topa Tim preserves the remains of a monastery and stupa, which seem to resemble those of Mauri Tim and are tentatively assigned to the third century.

In addition to these eroding vestiges there is evidence of rock-cut remains in the Kashgar Oasis; again, though none of these can compete with the monumental caves at Dunhuang and Kizil, they are amongst the oldest in Central Asia. Barely

more than 10 kilometres north of Kashgar is the Grotto of the Three Immortal Buddhas of the Han dynasty period (206 BC–AD 220). This consists of three small rectangular holes crudely excavated into the side of a vertical cliff, with no visible means of access. According to one investigator, who managed to reach the caves by means of a rope ladder, these rock-cut sanctuaries may be dated to the third or fourth century. However, they were partly restored during the seventeenth or eighteenth century, under the Qing period of influence in the Kashgar region, at which time what remained of their murals seems to have been vandalized. One cave apparently had seventy small, stucco Buddha figures, but these have vanished without a trace.

Little visited and barely protected by the authorities, Mauri Tim, Khan-oi and Topa Tim have until now not attracted the scholarly attention they deserve, considering they are the earliest vestiges of civilization in the Kashgar Oasis. It is not uncommon to come across previously protected sites that have been resold by local governments to peasants, who have then cultivated the grounds. The visible manifestations of early Buddhist cultures in Kashgar represents, moreover, only a small percentage of many other important sites that remain buried in the sands of Kashgar. Perhaps up to six Buddhist cities existed in this area into the tenth century. Local legends speak of religious wars between Buddhist and Islamic kings, caused by sectarian divisions that often split entire families and gave rise to so much bloodshed that today's farmers still believe that the soils of Khan-oi are fertile because of all the human remains in the area. When the sands of the Taklimakan blow vigorously in one direction, ruins are frequently uncovered, but they subsequently sink again as the winds blow in another direction. It can only be hoped that future archaeological research will eventually focus on these fascinating sites, so as to uncover their original form and purpose.

Of the two eroding, mud brick stupas at Mauri Tim, only one has portions of its hemispherical dome still preserved (above); even more decayed are the remains of a royal citadel at the nearby site of Khan-oi (right).

The Grotto of the Three Immortal Buddhas presents a line of small rock-cut doorways high up on a cliff face, now without any means of access.

TRAVELLERS' REPORTS

HIUEN TSANG
Chinese Buddhist pilgrim, 629

The country of Kie-sha [Kashgar] is about 5,000 li in circuit. It has much sandy and stony soil, and very little loam. It is regularly cultivated and is productive. Flowers and fruits are abundant. Its manufactures are a fine kind of twilled haircloth, and carpets of a fine texture and skilfully woven. The climate is soft and agreeable; the winds and rain regularly succeed each other. The disposition of the men is fierce and impetuous, and they are mostly false and deceitful. They make light of decorum and politeness, and esteem learning but little. Their custom is when a child is born to compress his head with a board of wood. Their appearance is common and ignoble. They paint their bodies and around their eyelids. For their writing they take their model from India, and although [the shapes of the letters] are somewhat mutilated, yet they are essentially the same in form. . . . They have a sincere faith in the religion of Buddha, and give themselves earnestly to the practice of it. There are several hundreds of sangharamas [monasteries], with some 10,000 followers; they study the Little Vehicle [sect of Buddhism] and belong to the Sarvastivada school.

Buddhist Records of the Western World
Translated from the Chinese of Hiuen Tsiang by Samuel Beal
(AD 629), Motilal Banarsidas, Delhi, 1981: pp. 306–7

MARCO POLO
Italian traveller, 1270s

At length you reach a place called Kashcar [Kashgar], which, it is said, was formerly an independent kingdom, but is now subject to the dominion of the Great Khan. Its inhabitants are of the Mahometan [Muslim] religion. The province is extensive, and contains many towns and castles, of which Kashcar is the largest and most important. The language of the people is peculiar to themselves. They subsist by commerce and manufacture, particularly works of cotton. They have handsome gardens, orchards and vineyards. Abundance of cotton is produced there, as well as flax and hemp. Merchants from this country travel to all parts of the world; but in truth they are a wretched, sordid race, eating badly and drinking worse. Besides the Mahometans there are amongst the inhabitants several Nestorian Christians, who are permitted to live under their own laws and to have their churches. The extent of the province is five days' journey.

The Travels of Marco Polo
Revised from Marsden's translation and edited with introduction by Manuel Komroff, Jonathan Cape, London, 1934: pp. 90–91

ROBERT SHAW,
Trader and traveller, first Englishman to enter Kashgar, 1869

We passed through a populous and well-cultivated country, crossing about four rivers during the day's ride. . . . On the banks of the last stream we stopped for the afternoon prayer. The fortress or new city of Kashgar was here in full sight, in the midst of an open treeless country, covered, however, with cultivation. The defences, as we approached, were seen to be exactly similar to those of Yarkand New City, but the place is smaller. Passing several obtuse angles of the wall, we reached a gate on the E.N.E. side, before which, however, we were met by a Yoozbashee [guard] carrying a double-barrelled rifle of European make. He and the Mahrambasee preceded us through the gate, past a corps de garde, where sat rows of soldiers [converted Chinese], through a second gate to the right past more rows of soldiers, and into a third gateway giving entrance into the New City. . . .

Jooma [Shaw's servant], by permission, went to the Old City. Says it is larger than Yarkand, and crowded every inch. The stables are underground, and all the houses have upper stories. The city has five gates, of which Jooma visited three. Hazrat Apak is nearly two miles off, beyond the city. No English print to be seen; Russian sells at from five to eight tillahs per piece of forty Kashgar guz [= thirty-one yds]. Indian tea, of which Jooma took a sample, was valued at forty tungas per jing [= thirty tungas per lb] about ten shillings a pound! He visited three shops where 'samovars' were kept boiling for selling hot cups of tea. With regard to cotton goods, they say they are dearer than usual, as the caravans from Russian are stopped. . . .

Half-a-dozen of the male prisoners and three little girls aged from five to fourteen were brought to my outer courtyard to be fitted with clothes by the Chinese tailors, who are engaged there at work for the Sirkar [or comptroller of stores]. The Yoozbashee says that thieves have been put down with a strong hand by the Atalik-Ghazee. Many have been hung and impaled; if even the value of a knife is stole, the thief is hung. . . .

Atalik-Ghazee has abolished the slave trade in his dominions. Formerly, there were regular markets where you could go and buy a boy or a girl or a grown-up slave; some sold for debt, some the prize of forays made against the neighbouring Sheeah tribes [Mahammadan heretics]. Now, household slaves still exist, but the trade is done away with, and the markets closed.

Visits to High Tartary, Yarkand and Kashgar
J. Murray, London, 1871; reprint Bhavana Books & Prints, New Delhi, 1996: pp. 258, 287, 336, 347

CHARLES ADOLPHUS MURRAY, 7TH EARL OF DUNMORE

English traveller, 1892

Amongst other excursions that I made in the neighbourhood of Kashgar, was one to the Mosque of Hazret Afarc [tomb of Apa Khoja] who was looked upon more as a saint than a sovereign by his people in this province, and who was buried in this mosque in AD 1693. Riding out of the city by the Northgate, or the Yarwakh Darwaza, Macartney and I proceeded for about two and a half miles in a northerly direction, passing through a vast cemetery, very well kept and containing some handsome tombs. This enormous graveyard lay to the right and left of the road for at least a mile and a half, and extended as far as the mosque, and thousands of tombs lay all around its outer walls. The mosque is a handsome building with a tower at each of its four corners, being topped with a large dome covered with green-glazed tiles. Each tower is cased in green and yellow tiles in broad alternate stripes, while its walls and the sides of its gracefully arched porch are also faced with tiles of blue and white patterns, much resembling those constantly to be met with in the old Moorish houses in Algiers. The mosque is surrounded on two sides, by a grove of the handsome Tarik tree, one or two of which were very fine specimens. Over the porch, where the top of the arch meets the line of flat-topped roofs which form the support for the dome, were two large ibex heads, and on the top of the wall which surrounds the building was a veritable chevaux-de-frise, composed of the horns of Ovis

Poli, ibex and other wild animals. Facing the centre of each wall outside the building were four altars, also built of green tiles, on which were piled hundreds of horns pyramidally. This custom seems to prevail over all this part of Central Asia, as we have come across many such pyramids of skulls and horns, in various places, commencing in Western Tibet and in the Kuen-lun mountains, as well as in the Pamirs.

The Pamirs: A Narrative of a Year's Expedition on Horseback and on Foot through Kashmir, Western Tibet, Chinese Tartary and Russian Central Asia
J. Murray, London 1893; reprint Bhavana Books & Prints, New Delhi, 2001: pp. 222–3

SIR AUREL STEIN

British explorer and archaeologist, 1900

Opal [a town in the Kashgar Oasis] is a conglomeration of numerous hamlets spread between fields and irrigated meadows. To ride along its lanes shaded by willows and poplars was a delightful change after the dreary wilderness of stone and sand we had lately passed through. In the fields the melons were ripening, and richly cultivated gardens displayed a profusion of vegetables. Everywhere was the welcome presence of water, irrigation cuts of all sizes following and intersecting the roads. The quantity of reddish mud deposited by these little streams was a notable feature. By the side of one I made a brief halt to refresh myself with a modest 'tiffin' carried in a saddle-bag and some apples and plums I had bought from a wayside stall. It was the first fruit I had tasted for months.

I can only briefly mention the remains of ancient structures which were the object of my first short excursions in the vicinity. Considering that the site of Kashgar in all probability corresponds to that of the capital of the ancient territory of 'Kie-sha', which Hiuen-Tsang describes as possessing hundreds of Buddhist monasteries, the remains of the pre-Muhammadan period still traceable above ground are scanty indeed. The most conspicuous is a much-decayed mound of sun-dried brick masonry [Mauri Tim] rising over the deep-cut northern bank of the Tumen-Darya, about a mile and a half to the north-west of Chini-Bagh, which undoubtedly represents the remains of a large Stupa. The present height of the mound is 85 feet, and the diameter of its base from east to west about 160 feet. But notwithstanding the exact survey made I found it impossible to ascertain the original form of the whole Stupa, or even to fix its centre, to such an extent have the masses of soft brick-work fallen or crumbled away. It was for me an instructive observation to find that fully 15 feet of the masonry base now lie below the level of the irrigated fields close by. ...

Beyond the garden stretched barren, sun-baked ground, filled with graves and tombs in all stages of decay. In its centre rises the simple but massive cupola which covers the resting-place of the holy Mairyam (Miriam) [in/outside Kashgar?]. Yaqub Beg, or Bedaulat as he is popularly known, had raised it with hard-burnt bricks, and the good condition of the building, which has seen no repairs since the death of its founder, speaks well for the solidity of the construction. All around are only crumbling ruins, mud walls slowly mingling with the loess dust from which they were made. The shrine has kept some of the land left to it by former pious benefactors, but it would be against all Eastern notions if any of the proceeds were spent on repairs. The feeding of poor pilgrims and of the ever-present Darwishes is a more urgent task.

Sand-Buried Ruins of Khotan: Personal Narrative of a Journey of Archaeological and Geographical Exploration in Chinese Turkestan
Hurst and Blackett, London, 1904; reprint Asian Educational Services, New Delhi, 2000: pp. 110, 124, 134

FILIPPO DE FILIPPI
Italian explorer, 1913

The city of Kashgar, like Yarkand, is surrounded by walls, but it is somewhat smaller in circumference. It is not the 'Cascar' or Casigar' of Marco Polo; that was destroyed at the beginning of the 16th century by Mirza Aba Bakr, and its ruins, called Eski Shahr, are 14 or 15 miles east of the present city. . . .

Kashgar is a large congeries of one-storied mud-brick houses, huddled together with scarcely any space for alleys and street. Flat-terraced roofs alternate with the quadrangular openings formed by the courtyards; or with tumble-down walls above which rise the facade of a mosque or medresse [madrasa], with turreted corners and a large pointed arch in the centre of the door. In the bazaar, however, the streets are fairly wide. It is a simple village market as at Yarkand; a few Russian and English goods are to be had, but they are of no great value. The people of Kashgar, however, made a better showing than those we had hitherto seen, and seemed both healthier and more prosperous.

The Italian Expedition to the Himalayas, Karakoram and Eastern Turkestan (1913–1914)
Edward Arnold, London 1932: pp. 486–8

CAPTAIN, L.V.S. BLACKER
British secret agent, 1918

Outside of Kashgar, far out among the Taklamakan desert dunes, there is a large area with tombs of holy men, memories from the time when an advancing Islam had fought the Buddhists who ruled Kashgar at the time. The largest and most important of the tombs bears the name Ordam-padishah, which is also the name of the whole region. During the prescribed time for pilgrimage, Kashgar's religious population, tens of thousands of men, women and children, went out to the desert to visit the tombs. They walked in long processions, carrying flags and banners and rags attached to long poles of poplar. They shouted and sang and praised and honoured the holy men. They were Kashgar's most fanatical believers in pilgrimage, a meritorious act, which if repeated often enough was equal to a pilgrimage to the far distant and less accessible Mecca. They were so fanatical that non-believers had to keep out of the way.

'The Guides': On Secret Patrol in High Asia
J. Murray, London 1922: pp. 113

C.P. SKRINE
British Consul-General, 1922

One's first impression on arrival at the Consulate General is of greenery and shade; of limes and acacias, willows and planes and fruit-trees of all kinds; of tall busy poplars rising like a wall against the sun, . . . of confused gardens on three different levels, with an orchard and a vine-pergola . . . and a carved Chinese summer-house, all mixed up with trees and an amazing riot of flowers and vegetables. . . . Stepping out on to the long terrace with its sundial and parapet of sun-dried brick, you find yourself on the top of a low bluff looking out over the wide shallow valley of the Tümen River. Immediately below you are the trees of the lower garden and its enclosing wall; then comes a narrow road-way with country people going to and from the busy town all day long; beyond it a patch of melon-beds and willow-fringed rice-fields, . . . Then comes the winding river, brimming in summer with the melted snows of the Tien Shan. On the further bank more rice-fields and a line of loess bluffs, below which here and there nestle cottages and water-mills buried in willows; beyond, trees and farmsteads stretch away to the northern edge of the oasis five miles distant, where in stark contrast a great sweep of gravelly desert slopes down to form the curiously-corrugated foothills of the Tien Shan. . . .

Perfectly clear weather is, alas, rare in Kashgaria owing to the fine loess dust which almost always thickens the atmosphere; but at two seasons of the year, early summer and later autumn, the atmosphere in the mornings could be clear as crystal and the farthest mountains plainly visible. . . .

From south right round by west to north-east they stretched, the walls that screen Kashgar from the rest of Asia. To the north indeed the snowless outer ranges of the Tien Shan were not impressive. . . . But right across the south-western horizon, sixty to a hundred miles away, stretched a mighty rampart of eternal snow. . . . It was the Kashgar Range, a hundred miles long and from 18,000 to 25,000 feet high, which walls the lofty table-land of the Pamirs from deserts and oases of the Tarim Basin.
Chinese Central Asia
Methuen, London, 1927; reprint Barnes & Noble, New York, 1971: pp. 55–7

LADY MACARTNEY
Wife of Sir George Macartney, British Consul-General, 1931

There are two Kashgar cities, the one being the old or Muhammadan City, with 40,000 inhabitants, though the Chinese Civil Administration is carried on there. . . . The T-tai, who is a sort of Provincial Commander-in-Chief, has his residence in the Chinese New City, where most of the troops are kept, though a small quote is quartered in the Old City.

The New City is seven miles to the South of the Old, and is smaller; the population being almost entirely Chinese. Both cities are walled in by enormous thick crenellated walls, in which are four massive iron gates, which are shut at sunset, and opened at daybreak, to the blowing of horns and firing of guns. And both cities are surrounded by wide moats, which look imposing, though I don't believe they are ever filled. Probably if they were, the water would melt the foundations of the wall, which seem to be simply of mud or of unbaked brick.

The two Consulates [British and Russian], and later the Russo-Asiatic Bank, and the Swedish Mission Station, were outside the walls of the Old City.

The streets of the Muhammadan City were very narrow and dirty, with ground all ups and downs, and mostly muddy from the water slopped over from the pails of the donkeys and water carriers. Dark little shops lined the streets, in some places made darker by the covering or awning of reed mats that were erected right across the road for shade. The shop-keepers squatted in the midst of their goods, and never seemed particularly anxious for customers. Just inside the gate, and along the street leading to the central bazaar, the beggars congregated, and most horrible

sights many of them were, with their faces and limbs eaten away and distorted with the most frightful diseases.

The narrow bazaars seemed to be always crowded, and especially so on Thursdays, the Bazaar-Kun, or Market Day. Then it was a slow business to push one's way through the throng of people, some on foot, others mounted on donkeys and horses, animals so loaded with fodder that only a nose and four hoofs could be seen, and caravans of camels and horses, carrying great hard bales of cotton. The bells the camels wore always sounded to me so like a peal of church bells that sometimes on a Sunday morning, when sitting in the garden, hearing the camels down at the river, I closed my eyes and felt as though I was at home and it was church time.

The main streets seemed mostly to run into the big Market Square known as the Id-ga, in the centre of which stood the Chief Mosque. On Friday morning all the men went there, dressed in their best, to say their prayers, and from the roof of this Mosque we heard from our house at intervals during the day, the Mullah's call to prayer. . . .

I wish I could adequately describe the beauty and picturesqueness of the Id-ga bazaar, as seen from the steps of the Mosque. In the centre of the great square were the fruit stalls; in summer piled high with fruit, crimson peaches, apricots, mulberries, enormous bunches of black and white grapes and purple and yellow figs. . . . Then there were melons of so many varieties, some being cut open to show the inside. . . .

Then the Cap stalls gave a wonderfully pretty touch of colour. They looked like flowers on their stands. Bright coloured velvet caps of every hue, some lined and trimmed with fur for winter, others gaily embroidered for summer wear, and round which a turban could be wound for full dress; and some decorated with patterns of silver beaten thin and sewn on; these were for the women to wear on high days and holidays. The people too were all dressed in the brightest of colours. . . . The brilliant shades suited them and their surroundings so perfectly.

The side streets were often given up to one special trade, and so you found the Cotton bazaar, the Chintz bazaar, where the Russian prints were sold, the Blacksmiths' and Silversmith's bazaars, the flour and grain bazaars, and so on. And one horrible place went by the name of the flea bazaar, for it was there that the old clothes were sold, and I am pretty certain that it lived up to its name.

Of course, the inevitable tea shop, or Chai-Khana, was everywhere, where people sat and drank tea while they listened to dreamy native music played by a band consisting of perhaps one or two long-necked mandolin-shaped instruments that produced very soft fair-like music, accompanied by a small drum. Or they listened to a professional story teller. . . .

Many of the shops had a wicker birdcage hanging up, in which was a red-legged partridge, called a Kek-lik, so named for the sound he made, or a ground lark which continued a shrill, trilling song. . . .

The people of Kashgar are of many different types. Tall, handsome, aristocratic-looking men and women, with almost European features, rosy-cheeked and flat-faced people of the Kirghiz type, Afghans with their thin, sharp profiles, natives of India, both Hindu and Muhammadan, and Chinese. One met too, fair-haired and blue-eyed people, showing possibly their unmixed Aryan descent. One could hardly say what the real Kashgar type was, for it has become so mixed by the invasion of other peoples in the past. Many of the women were very attractive, and some of the children extraordinarily handsome, especially the dark-eyed boys and girls of about twelve, who looked quite Italian or Spanish in their velvet coats and tight-fitting caps.

An English Lady in Chinese Turkestan
Ernest Benn, London, 1931; reprint Oxford University Press, Hong Kong, 1999: pp. 62–8

GEORGES LE FEVRE
French traveller, 1931–2

The terrace of the hospitable British Consulate looked out upon an Arcadia in which, so far as the eye could reach, stretched cultivated fields, gardens, vineyards, and groves of lime and plane trees, acacias and willows. Beyond, to the north were the Celestial Mountains; to the south the far distant peaks of the Kashgar Range. It was indeed, a land of promise. Not far from the British Consulate, and almost facing it, was that of the Soviet; but it was difficult to say which Power exercised the predominating influence in Kashgaria. In 1913 Russian troops tried to occupy the region, and a representative of the Tsar established his headquarters at Tashkurghan. The Tao-Tai let events take their course, and three months later the intruder died of a strange sickness – poisoned, it was said – and the Chinese gently reassumed control.

An Eastern Odyssey, The Third Expedition of Haardt and Audouin-Dubreil
Little, Brown and Company, Boston 1935: pp. 226–7

DIANA SHIPTON
Wife of the Consul-General in Kashgar, 1947

The colour of soft brown loess dust predominates [in the Kashgar Oasis]. The earth, the roads, the houses, the rough 'bricks' drying in the sun, the massive, fortified walls of Kashgar city, the graves, so carefully built, so soon crumbling back into the ground, are all the same uniform colour.

It rains so seldom that there is no need to build solid, efficient houses, . . . the native houses rise up from the earth from which they are built, loose and casual. . . . Only mosques are given more care and attention. They are clean and upright, with carved pillars of wood and lattice work windows.

The great walls of Kashgar, raised at intervals to a massive watch-tower, overlook the ant-like activity of the bazaar on one side, and the leisurely life of the roads and the irrigated fields on the other. Only the bridges, with their arches overhead, and the one Chinese Temple, standing high in the city, with its typical up-tilting roof, mark conspicuously the foreign rule.

Normally the Kashgar scene is essentially a Turki one. The hidden women, the bearded, weak-faced men, so surprisingly fair skinned, the fleets of donkeys, the creaking wooden carts with extraordinarily insecure-looking wheels, the gayly caparisoned mappa ponies with their bells, the little girls with their innumerable tiny pigtails and round, embroidered caps, a boy wandering along playing on a flute, the melon sellers by the road-side – all these are typical and essentially Turki.

The Antique Land
Hodder and Stoughton, London 1950: pp. 133–5

NOTES

1. Colin Makerras (1972), *The Uighur Empire According to the T'ang Dynastic Histories*, University of South Carolina Press, Columbia, SC..

2. Hiuen Tsang (629), *Buddhist Records of the Western World*, Translated from Chinese by Samuel Beal, Motilal Banarsidas, Delhi, 1983, pp.306-307.

3. Mahmud al Kashgari (1941), *Divanu Lugat-it Turk, Tipkibasimt: 'Faksimie'*, Ed. Besim Atalay, Alaeddin Kiral Basmevi, Ankara.

4. Hodong Kim (2004), *Holy War in China: The Muslim Rebellion and State in Chinese Central Asia*, 1964-1877, Stanford University Press, California.

5. The 'Great Game' had its origins in the 1860s when the expansion of the Russian Empire into Central Asia caused the British to fear the security of their Indian Empire which had already been challenged by the Indian Mutiny of 1857: see Karl E Meyer and Shareen Blair Brysac (2006), *Tournament of Shadows: The Great Game and the Race for Empire in Central Asia, Basic Books*, New York, pp.137-169.

6. Ayxem Eli (2006), '*Gender, Social Hierarchy and Ethnicity – a case study of urban Kashgar, XUAR, China*', Ph.D. thesis the University of Melbourne, Australia, pp.44-58 on the social hierarchies of Kashgar.

7. Marika Vicziany and Guibin Zhang (2007), 'Minority entrepreneurs on the move: the Uygurs' in Ingrid Neilson, Russell Smyth and Marika Vicziany (eds.) (2007), *Globalisation and Labour Mobility in China, Monash University Press*, Melbourne, pp.53-73.

8. Major H W Bellew (1875), *Kashmir and Kashgar: a narrative of the journey of the embassy to Kashgar in 1873-1874*, Trubner and Co., London, pp.367-378; Gunnar Jarring (1935) 'The Ordam-Padishah-system of Eastern Turkistan Shrines', Geografiska Annaler, vol. 17, Supplement, 348-354.

9. A rare book we came across in Chinese language on the subject of Uygur architecture in Kashgar and Xinjiang more generally is: Hasan Abdul Rahim (1989), *Xinjiang Ancient Architecture and Art*, Xinjiang Xinhua Press, Urumuqi.

SELECT BIBLIOGRAPHY

Asian Development Bank, *The 2020 Project: Policy Support in the People's Republic of China: Final Report and Policy Directions, Manila, 2003* http://www.adb.org/Documents/Reports/2020_Project/default.asp.

Barfield, T. *The Perilous Frontier: Nomadic Empires and China*, Basil Blackwell, Oxford, 1989.

Boulnois, Luce, *Silk Road: Monks, Warriors and Merchants on the Silk Road*, Airphoto International Ltd, London, 2004.

Heissing, Walther, *The Religions of Mongolia*, translated from German by Geoffrey Samuel, Kegan Paul International, London and New York, 2000.

Kim, Hodong, *Holy War in China: The Muslim Rebellion and State in Chinese Central Asia, 1864–1877*, Stanford University Press, California, 2004.

Macartney, Lady, *An English Lady in Chinese Turkestan* (London 1931 first edition), reprinted Oxford University Press, Hong Kong, 1985.

Mackerras, Colin, *The Uighur Empire: According to the T'ang Dynastic Histories*, University of South Carolina Press, Columbia, SC, 1972.

Rahim, Hasan Abdul, Xinjiang *Ancient Architecture and Art*, *Xinjiang* Xinhua Press, Urumqi, 1989 (in Chinese).

Shaw, Robert, *Visits to High Tartary, Yarkand and Kashgar* (London 1871 first edition), reprinted Bhavana Books & Prints, New Delhi, 1996.

Stein, M. Aurel, *Sand-Buried Ruins of Khotan: Personal Narrative of a Journey of Archaeoological and Geographical Exploration in Chinese Turkestan* (London 1904 first edition), reprinted Asian Educational Services, New Delhi/Madras, 2000.

Whitefield, Susan, *Aurel Stein on the Silk Road*, The British Museum Press, London, 2004.

Wood, Frances, *The Silk Road: Two Thousand Years in the Heart of Asia*, The British Library, London, 2004.

ACKNOWLEDGEMENTS

This photographic essay is the work of the Kashgar Project Team that was established in the Monash Asia Institute at Monash University, Melbourne, in 2004. From the beginning, our team worked with Professor Tsui Yen Hu at the Xinjiang Normal University in Urumqi. This collaboration has now resulted in the establishment of a joint Old Silk Road Project between the Monash Asia Institute and the Oasis Institute at the Xinjiang Normal University. During the last four years, Professor Tsui Yen Hu contributed not only his expertise but also critical logistical support to our work in Xinjiang. Special thanks are also due to the Department of Tourism and Department of Foreign Relations (Xinjiang Government, PRC) for giving us permission to undertake this work in Kashgar and offering their enthusiastic support. We hope that foreign tourists will now be encouraged to spend more time visiting Kashgar and creating new employment that is urgently needed in this part of western China.

The brilliance and generosity of John Gollings must at the outset be acknowledged. John joined the team at the start and has continued to work on his inspirational photographs. During the first period of fieldwork in March-April 2005, John took no less than 7,000 photographs in the Kashgar Prefecture over a period of three weeks, of which only a small fraction have been included in this volume. John Gollings has an international reputation for his remarkable photographs of Vijayanaga in south India. I am certain that his work on Kashgar will become equally well known.

George Michell is the other critical factor in this work. Best known for his writings on Indian architectural history and art – in particular his remarkable work on Vijayanagara - George's expertise has been invaluable. He has been a meticulous co-author and delightful project partner at every point. George introduced us to John Gollings, the publisher Frances Lincoln and to our wonderful publishing agent Anne Engel. We thank them all.

The selection of the photographs was greatly assisted by Esa Epstein and her staff at Sepia International Inc., New York. We are grateful to her for this. Special appreciation is reserved for John Nicoll, Gillian Greenwood and Andrew Dunn of Frances Lincoln in London for their attention to detail and enthusiasm for publishing a book about a city that has been greatly ignored during the last hundred years. The historical photographs of Kashgar on pages 10, 12, 13, 14, and 15 are reproduced here with the permission of the British Library, custodians of a large section of the Sir Aurel Stein Collection. We thank Susan Whitfield, for her encouragement from the start.

Behind the photographer and the authors of this work stands a talented team of scholarly specialists without whom the research on Kashgar would not have been possible: Dr Andrea Di Castro (Monash Asia Institute) is a scholar of Asian art and archaeology; Dr Ayxe Eli (Max Planck Institute) is a specialist on contemporary Uygur language and culture; Dr Faridullah Bezhan (Monash Asia Institute) is a scholar of Persian culture and history; Ablikem (Xinjiang Normal University) acted as an invaluable translator; Nicki Medlik (author & designer for Thames & Hudson) acted as John's photographic assistant in China and advised us on the final selection of photographs for this collection; Diana Cousens (Monash Asia Institute) helped to collate the Travellers' Tales. The Kashgar Project Team has continued to grow and we have benefited by the insights provided by new members with expertise in the fields of IT, geography and mapping, especially Tom Chandler, Dr Xuan Zhu, Uri Gilad and Assoc. Prof. Jim Petersen all from Monash University. Uri Gilad also prepared the sketch on pp.6–7. This project has also benefited greatly from the advice and enthusiasm of Dr Leanna Darvall (Medical School, Monash University) and Professor John Olsen (University of Arizona).

Each member of the Kashgar team is engaged in writing separate monographs about Kashgar from their unique perspective – we look forward to the publication of all these works. My own interest in Kashgar began in 2001 during my first period of fieldwork in western China on a research project for the Asian Development Bank and the State Council of China. My enthusiasm for Kashgar continues to grow and I thank all those people who have made my memorable visits possible.

Marika Vicziany (Kashgar Team Leader)
Director, Monash Asia Institute
Monash University, Melbourne, Australia, April 2008

The photographer John Gollings riding to the Sunday Market in a donkey cart.